Chattahoochee River National Recreation Area

Allenbrook

Historic Structure Report

2004

Hartrampf, Inc.

and

Office of Jack Pyburn, Architect, Inc.

for

Historical Architecture, Cultural Resources Division

Southeast Regional Office

National Park Service

The historic structure report presented here exists in two formats. A traditional, printed version is available for study at the park, the Southeastern Regional Office of the NPS (SERO), and at a variety of other repositories. For more widespread access, the historic structure report also exists in a web- based format through ParkNet, the website of the National Park Service. Please visit www.nps.gov for more information.

Cultural Resources
Southeast Region
National Park Service
100 Alabama St. SW
Atlanta, GA 30303
(404) 562-3117

2004
Historic Structure Report
Allenbrook
Chattahoochee River National Recreation Area
Atlanta, GA
LCS#: 091884

Allenbrook
Historic Structure Report
2004

Approved by: _Kevin G. Cheri_   _11/29/04_
Superintendent, Chattahoochee National Recreation Area   Date

Recommended by: _____   _12-8-04_
Chief, Cultural Resource Division   Date
Southeast Region

Recommended by: _____   _12-8-04_
Associate Regional Director, Cultural Resource   Date
Stewardship and Partnership, Southeast Region

Approved by: _____   _12-10-04_
Regional Director, Southeast Region   Date

Table of Contents

Project Team

Hartrampf, Inc.

Robert A. Bass, P.E., President, Project Manager

Deborah Harvey, Historian and Project Coordinator

The Office of Jack Pyburn, Architect, Inc.

Jack Pyburn, AIA, President, Historical Architect

Jacqueline Renell, Preservation Planner and Architectural Historian

Jay Carlson, Field Measurements and Graphics

Brandy Herlinger, Drafter

Foreword

We are pleased to make available this historic structure report, as part of our ongoing effort to provide comprehensive documentation for the historic structures and landscapes of National Park Service units in the Southeast Region. The authors would like to thank Kevin Cheri, Superintendent of the Chattahoochee River National Recreation Area, and his staff, especially David Ek, for their helpful aid in compiling this report. They opened their files for the authors' use; cheerfully provided access, including ladders, to the building; and provided thoughtful comment on the draft versions of the report. Dr. David McCreery, Professor of History at Georgia State University, also reviewed a draft of the historical portions of this document and suggested appropriate improvements. The staff at the Roswell Historical Society Archives, guided by Elaine DeNiro, archivist, were also extremely helpful in unearthing information. Two volunteers, Burt Terrell and Aubrey Morris, were particularly helpful, patiently locating any requested information and making suggestions for acquiring what they could not find. The authors would also like to thank Tommy Jones of the Southeastern Regional Office for his helpful comments and review of this material. It is our hope that this study of Allenbrook will prove valuable to park management in its ongoing efforts to preserve the building and to everyone in understanding and interpreting this unique resource.

Dan Scheidt
Chief, Cultural Resources Division
Southeast Regional Office
2004

Management Summary

In 1994, Historical Architect Ali Miri, of the National Park Service Southeast Regional Office, completed a Historic Structure Assessment Report for Allenbrook. Between 1998 and the present, the National Park Service has undertaken major renovations of the building, prompting this Historic Structure Report. The aim of this report is to expand upon earlier reports, both in historical inquiry and in reporting of physical condition, and to provide more detailed recommendations to the National Park Service for the preservation, restoration, rehabilitation, interpretation, and use of this historic building.

Methodology

The contract for this Historic Structure Report restricted the amount of background research for this report to only the information provided by the National Park Service. However, a limited amount of other research was deemed necessary for better understanding of the historic context of this property. Therefore, there may be material and information still in public or private hands that has not been reviewed for this report. In preparation for this report, Hartrampf, Inc. received copies of prior reports on Allenbrook and the Ivy Mills from the National Park Service. Jacqueline Renell, of The Office of Jack Pyburn, Architect, Inc., also visited the offices of the Chattahoochee River National Recreational Area and obtained copies of other pertinent documents. Some of these documents were completed under the auspices of the National Park Service, and others were compiled for other governmental agencies. These documents were supplemented with some historical background research conducted on the Internet, inquiry in the census archives for the area, a visit to the Roswell Historical Society Archives, and a review of the minutes of the Roswell Manufacturing Company housed in the DeKalb History Center Archives.

The project team conducted several site visits to Allenbrook for the purpose of taking photographs and measurements to aid in the physical description and assessment of the property. The first site visit was made on September 11, 2003, four more site visits were made October through December, 2003, and two final visits were made in May and June of 2004.

Draft versions of this report were submitted to the National Park Service for review at the 75% and 95% complete milestones, and comments, changes, and additional information was incorporated into the 95% and Final submittal reports. The contract for this report also allowed for only a limited discussion of treatment and use. Therefore, recommendations have been included for further research that will be necessary for a full understanding of the Allenbrook property and its relationship to its historic surroundings.

Historical Summary

Roswell King and some of his family moved to the area about 1838 and, with six other families from the Darien, Georgia area, established the town of Roswell, purchasing the land on which Allenbrook now stands. With his son, Barrington King, Roswell King built or purchased mills on Vickery Creek that included a cotton mill, a saw mill, a woolen mill, a flour mill, and a brick kiln. These were incorporated as the Roswell Manufacturing Company. Roswell King died in 1844, but his son continued to develop the mill industries of Roswell.

One important issue for this report is to establish a clearer definition of the date of construction. Based on significant but circumstantial evidence, this report concludes that James R. King probably built Allenbrook between 1851 and 1856 for his own use. The materials and construction methods define the building as an ante-bellum structure. Barrington King sold the property on which Allenbrook was built to his son, James R. King, in 1852. On part of this property, James and his brother, Thomas King, built the Ivy Mill at the confluence of Vickery Creek and the Chattahoochee River. James King married in 1851, and it is likely that he built Allenbrook to house his family. The building is located near enough to Ivy Mill to allow him to oversee the facility, but far enough to provide spatial separation between the owner of the mill and its workers. Although some writers suggest that Allenbrook was originally built to house workers at the Ivy Mill, the substantial nature of the structure, the fact that it is a two-story dwelling apparently intended for a single family, and the brick detailing, including the decorative treatment of the mortar between the bricks, indicate that the house was built for someone with a higher social standing than that of a mill worker, even an overseer, bookkeeper, or loom boss. Data from the census records corroborate that, in 1860, James King did not live near his father, Barrington King, who is enumerated near workers for the Roswell Manufacturing Company. In many cases, the census record specifies the place of employment for these workers as "RMC" or "RMCo." James R. King, on the other hand, is enumerated near workers at a woolen mill. Though the census record does not specify the name, the Ivy Woolen Mill was the only wool mill operating in the vicinity at the time. This data indicates that James King lived near the Ivy Mill, likely in the building now called Allenbrook.

Several writers state that John Brown, loom boss at the Ivy Mill, occupied Allenbrook with his wife, Mary, during the Civil War. While evidence suggests that this may be true, the occupation appears to have been a temporary measure precipitated by the Civil War and the need to leave someone responsible for the houses of the wealthy while their owners removed themselves to safer locations. The assertion by several writers that the house was built for, and occupied by, Theophile Rochè, who was managing the Ivy Mill when Federal forces arrived in Roswell in July of 1864, is false. Why that is so is detailed in the body of this report.

After the Civil War, the property on which Allenbrook stands passed out of the hands of the King family. It was included, though never specifically mentioned, in all deeds of sale of property associated with the Ivy Mill, later known as the Laurel Mill. In 1923, Georgia Power Company purchased the Laurel Mill property and Allenbrook. In 1932, the family of Barnett Allen Bell purchased from Georgia Power the portion of the property on which Allenbrook is located. It was they who named it Allenbrook. They undertook modernization of the house, adding plumbing and electricity, remodeling the interior, especially the upper level, changing the porch at the front of the house, and building a back stoop. On the grounds, they cleared away underbrush, created a front porch floor of brick salvaged from the Ivy Mill, and built a terrace of the same brick at the back of the house.

The Bells lived in the house until the 1970s. After Mr. Bell died, Mrs. Barnett A. Bell sold the property to the National Park Service in 1978 to be part of the new Chattahoochee River National Recreational Area, Vickery Creek Unit. For a time, the Roswell Historical Society occupied the building under agreement with the National Park Service. The Roswell Historical Society used Allenbrook as a headquarters and a Welcome Center to the City of Roswell. The Roswell Historical Society also made some modest changes to the building during their tenure. After the Roswell Historical Society removed from the building, the National Park Service undertook more substantial stabilization and restoration measures, especially during the period of 2000 to 2002.

Allenbrook is eligible for inclusion in the National Register of Historic Places, and should be listed. It is a culturally significant building, part of the early history of the City of Roswell, and associated with the Ivy Mill. It is also architecturally significant, as it is a rare example of a brick Plantation Plain style house that retains much of its original plan and character. The National Park Service wishes to use Allenbrook as an entry point to the Vickery Creek Unit of the Chattahoochee River National Recreation Area and to interpret its value and context to future generations of visitors.

Architectural Summary

Though Allenbrook retains many of its original Plantation Plain style features, several significant ones have been lost and other, non-contributing features have been added. On the exterior, the shadow of the earliest, hip-roofed porch is evident on the front. This porch was of frame construction with a brick pier foundation. After the Bells purchased the building, they removed the existing front porch. Over the ensuing years, they built a succession of porches at the front of the house. The first porch that the Bells built was a small, one-story porch at the front door with square columns, a gabled roof, and a small pad of brick salvaged from the old Ivy/Laurel Mill buildings. This involved the addition of a considerable amount of fill dirt at the front of the building to bring the level of the ground to within a few inches of the finished floor level of the main floor. They later removed this porch and built a two-story, full-length porch with square columns and a flat roof. The Bells also altered the back of the house. They removed a central doorway to the back of the house and installed a new one to the east, bricking up the original opening. They also installed a brick stoop on the back of the building, which provided access to the new rear door. By 1940, at least, this stoop was surrounded by a metal pipe handrail.

On the interior, the Bells renovated both the first and second floors. On the first floor, they blocked the north end of the hall with the construction of a bathroom, remodeled the stairway to the second floor and the entrance to the living room located in the southwestern corner of the house, constructed closets in the northern rooms, closed an opening into the dining room from under the stairs, and added new hearths and new mantels to two of the four fireplaces. They divided the upper level into three rooms, one of which was used as second bathroom, and two closets. In addition, the Bells installed kitchen and bath fixtures and introduced modern plumbing and electricity to the house.

In the 1980s, the Roswell Historical Society made changes to the building that included installation of gypsum board ceilings and recessed lighting as well as the painting of a floor cloth in the first floor hallway, although, at the time, the National Park Service was the owner of the property. After the Roswell Historical Society vacated the building, the National Park Service undertook extensive stabilization and rehabilitation that resulted in, among other things, new doors and hardware being installed on the exterior.

Overall, thanks to the stabilization measures undertaken by the National Park Service, Allenbrook appears to be in substantially good condition, with a few exceptions where repairs should still be made regardless of the treatment option selected. These would include repair of damaged window glass, treatment of deteriorated wood features where appropriate, repair of damaged wall surfaces, especially of the wall on the east side of the stairway, and repair of the water damaged ceilings.

Summary of Recommended Treatments

Based on the information revealed through the physical investigation and research for this report, it is recommended that the exterior of Allenbrook be restored to its pre-1932 appearance. In 1932, Barnett Allen Bell purchased the property from the owner of the Laurel Mill complex, the Georgia Power Company, for which Bell worked. By 1940, the house had been significantly renovated by the Bell family. According to historic photographs dated 1940 and the physical investigation for this report, the building had, by then, undergone many of the changes evident today. Along with the information revealed through research about the evolution of the interior, the photographs serve as a significant resource for interpreting the layers of history embodied within the house.

The two most significant events in the history of this house were the time of its original construction in the early 1850s as the dwelling of the owner of the Ivy Mill and its sale in 1932 to the Barnett A. Bell family. Between those two events, the building was consistently associated with the Ivy/Laurel Mill property, owned by the owner of the Ivy/Laurel Mills, and occupied by workers associated in some way with those mills. The first preference for interpretation is to return the house to its appearance in 1932, when it ceased to be legally associated with the Ivy/Laurel Mill property. Two watercolors painted by Barnett A. Bell of the front and back of the house in 1932 provide some information regarding the general appearance of the exterior of the house when purchased by the Bells. Investigation for this report revealed the likely interior configuration and some early finish treatments. However, returning the interior of the house to its 1932 appearance would cause the removal of a significant amount of material, which could result in damaging the earlier historic materials. Furthermore, the renovations undertaken by the Bells are historic in their own right. Therefore, it is recommended that restoration the pre-1932 period be limited to the exterior of the building and that the interior be preserved intact.

This recommendation involves reconstruction of the hipped-roof front porch as shown in the watercolor by Barnet A. Bell and as delineated by the shadow of the roofline on the front elevation of the house. Archaeological investigation should be undertaken to determine if any evidence remains of the brick piers originally supporting the porch. This investigation must be conducted to a minimum of three feet below the existing ground surface due to the extensive ground-disturbing activities that the front yard of the house has experienced over the past seventy-five years. At the back of the house, the existing stoop and porch roof should be removed. The existing door to Room 104 should be removed and a window matching the existing historic examples located elsewhere on the building should be installed, along with brick infill, in the opening. The historic door opening at the center of the rear elevation, where Window 5 now is, should be reinstated with a door similar to that depicted in Bell's watercolor installed in the opening. The watercolor depicts a wooden stair without handrails ascending to the opening on the exterior at this location. This should be reconstructed. However, because this stair does not meet code for public access, this door should be locked on the inside and should only be unlocked to provide egress in an emergency. Archaeological investigation should also be undertaken at the rear of the building to determine, if possible, the locations of early out-buildings. It is probable that the earliest arrange-ment of this site included both an exterior kitchen and a privy. While not known to have been in exist-ence at the time the Bell family purchased the house, locating their remains, if existing, would aid in reconstructing the physical history of the site. The interior of the building should be preserved as it is until the National Park Service determines a use for the structure. Options for use are discussed later in this report.

Allenbrook is an unusual and significant architec-tural feature of the Piedmont region in that it is a brick Plantation Plain style building that retains much of its original materials and configuration more than one hundred years after its construction. Most such houses, if they still exist, have been mod-ified beyond immediate recognition. The modifica-tions made to Allenbrook by the Bells did not entirely destroy the character of the building. Addi-tionally, the history of residential use, connecting Allenbrook to the King family, founders of the City of Roswell, and its continued affiliation with the local mills, make the building culturally significant to the area. For these reasons, restoration of the exterior to the pre-1932 period is the recommended treatment.

Administrative Data

Locational Data
Building Name: Allenbrook

Building Address: 227 South Atlanta Street, Roswell, GA 30075

LCS No.: 091884

Related Studies

Braley, Chad O., Karen G. Wood, and T. Jeffrey Price, *An Archeological and Historical Survey of a Fifteen Acre Tract in Roswell, Fulton County, Georgia,* Athens, GA: Southeastern Archeological Services, Inc., 1992.

Brown, Lenard E. "Historic Resource Study: Chattahoochee River National Recreation Area and the Chattahoochee River Corridor," Atlanta: Southeastern Regional Office, National Park Service, 1980.

Fulton County, Georgia, Gail D'Avino, preparer, *Assessment of No Adverse Effect to Allenbrook, the Robertson House, the H. S. Weaver House, the Roswell Historic National Register District and Ivy/Laurel Mill (Site 9FU228),* Atlanta: 1997.

Miri, Ali, *Historic Structure Assessment Report – Allenbrook House*. Atlanta: Historic Architecture Division, Southeast Region, National Park Service, 1994.

Wood, Karen, *An Archeological Survey of the Presumed Location of the First Roswell Factory*. Athens, GA: Southeastern Archeological Services, Inc., 1989.

Cultural Resource Data

National Register of Historic Places. Allenbrook has been recommended eligible for listing in the National Register of Historic Places. This recommendation, however, has not been confirmed by the State Historic Preservation Office. The Roswell Historical District was listed in the National Register of Historic Places in 1973. Allenbrook was not included in the boundaries of the District at the time. The Roswell Historic District was expanded in 1988 to include Allenbrook, but the expansion was never formally included in the National Register District. Considering its remote location and the number of intervening and non-contributing structures between Allenbrook and the rest of the National Register District, Allenbrook probably could not be included in the Roswell Historic District National Register listing. Allenbrook should be listed in the National Register of Historic Places as an individual resource under Criteria A, B, and C.

Period of Significance. A General Management Plan for this resource has not been completed. Therefore, a period of significance has not been determined. This report recommends that the Period of Significance be established as beginning when Allenbrook was constructed, between 1851 and 1856, and ending circa 1932, when the building ceased to be legally associated with the Ivy/Laurel Mill property.

Proposed Treatment and Use. Because a General Management Plan for this resource has not been completed, a treatment and use has not been estab-lished. According to National Park Service personnel, the proposed use is to interpret both the exterior surroundings and the interior of Allenbrook. However, this proposal may be incompatible with the location of the building as well as with staffing and resources available at the Park. Although located within the Historic District of Roswell, its addition was an afterthought, as the building is not physically within reasonable walking distance of the rest of the historic structures in the District and is separated from the District by a number of non-contributing structures. Therefore, its physical connection with the Roswell Historic District is tenuous, at best, though its cultural connection is strong. To ensure the ultimate protection of the building, a plan for continued occupancy would prove ideal. One option would be to use the building as a residence for a Park Service ranger at the Chattahoochee River National Recreation Area. Another use possibility would be as a classroom or museum facility, to host educational programs or exhibits. Although meeting the occupancy consideration, using Allenbrook for administrative office space would be the least optimal use given the impact such a function may have on the structural stability of the building. Until a use is determined, the recommended treatment of the interior is preservation. The interior should be preserved as it is, and only routine maintenance and repairs should be undertaken to prevent further deterioration of the historic materials. The exterior, however, should be restored to its pre-1932 appearance to enhance the connection of Allenbrook to the Ivy/Laurel Mill ruins that are now part of the Chattahoochee River National Recreation Area. The Park should institute a vigorous educational plan to actively engage a continuous flow of visitors to the Vickery Creek Unit to learn about the natural and cultural history of the area and to learn about the connection between the ruins and Allenbrook and their significance to Roswell and the South.

Historical Background and Context

The purpose of this section is to explore the background history of Allenbrook and its historical context. Various writers in the past proposed an assortment of theories on the date of construction, the purpose of construction, and the names of the occupants of this building. This report examines those theories in light of the most current evidence available to the researcher. The objective is to create a coherent, verifiable history from the fragments of past efforts, discarding those elements that do not withstand critical scrutiny.

As Union troops advanced upon Roswell, Georgia in July of 1864, Confederate Adjutant A. W. Harris wrote on behalf of Colonel M. H. Wright in Atlanta to the Captain of the Roswell Battalion, stationed in Roswell, to retreat across the Chattahoochee River toward Atlanta to avoid allowing their arms and ammunition to fall into the hands of the enemy.[1] James Roswell King, Captain of the Roswell Battalion and son of one of the founders of the Roswell Manufacturing Company, gave final instructions to his "head man" to keep the mills running "until driven out" by the soldiers.[2] Then, with his seventy- five men, he withdrew across the river and burned the bridge behind him. To keep the munitions from falling into the hands of the Union soldiers, he left Roswell and its collection of cotton, wool, and flour mills unprotected against the advancing army. All that remained to defend them were the elderly, the women and children who worked in the mills, two mill superintendents, and a few foreign workers. The Reverend Nathaniel Pratt, Presbyterian minister, also stayed behind to tend his flock and defend the homes of the wealthy owners of the mills, who earlier fled to Atlanta, Macon, Augusta, or Savannah.[3]

The men entrusted with the task of keeping the woolen mill running in the face of an advancing enemy, executed a desperate plan. They hoisted a French flag belonging to an employee and citizen of France, weaver Theophile Rochè, above the mill and continued operations.[4] When General Kenner Garrard of the Union Army marched into Roswell on July 6, 1864, Rochè claimed that he, a French national, was an owner of the mills and that the soldiers should not harm the mills since they operated under a neutral flag. This gambit worked until the next day when Garrard, inspecting the mills, observed the letters CSA woven into the cloth. He immediately closed the mills, removed large amounts of cloth, thread, and rope for the use of the Union Army, and ordered the mills burned. At the direction of General William Tecumseh Sherman, Garrard arrested the mill workers on charges of treason and marched them under guard to Marietta as prisoners of war, where Union soldiers put them on trains heading north.

In the years following the Civil War, many myths and legends grew up around this incident in Roswell. Most centered on the fate of the women of Roswell sent by the army to northern states. One, however, involved the French weaver, Theophile Rochè. Believed to be a central player in this drama, he acquired some status. His legend, therefore, required a locus, a place to hang his hat. The legend of Theophile Rochè eventually included assertions that he was the superintendent of the Ivy Mill and

---

1. Adjutant A. W. Harris to Captain James R. King, quoted in Michael Hitt, *Charged With Treason: Ordeal of 400 mill workers during military operations in Roswell, Georgia, 1864-1865,* Monroe, NY: Library Research Associates, Inc., 1992, p. 1.
2. James King, quoted in Hitt, p. 3.
3. Darlene M. Walsh, ed. *Roswell – A Pictorial History,* 2nd ed. (reprinted in 2000), Charlotte: Fine Books Publishing Company, 1994, p. 67.
4. Hitt, pp. 14. 16.

lived in the two-story brick house on Roswell Road located between the Ivy Mill and the Roswell Mills and now known as Allenbrook. The National Park Service purchased the property in 1978. By that time, the established history of Allenbrook was that a member of the King family, sometimes said to be Roswell King, built it in the mid-1840s as an office and residence for the manager of the Ivy Woolen Mill, often said to be Theophile Rochè.[5] Another writer added that Rochè owned the Allenbrook property.[6] Careful consideration of the available evidence shows that, while the established history contains elements of the truth, earlier writers rearranged and misapplied those elements to the point that this explanation of the construction of Allenbrook is false.

Allenbrook is surrounded by history and mystery. The date of construction is uncertain, the reason for constructing it is unclear, and many of the occupants before 1930 are undetermined. Over the years, Allenbrook did not attract the interest of most historians of the Roswell Mills and the city of Roswell, so it remained obscure except for the legend of Theophile Rochè. However, the history of the Roswell area provides clues to the possible construction date of Allenbrook and its purpose, as does analysis of the materials and construction methods used.

Also important to dating the structure are the building plan and details as they relate to other buildings in the Roswell area. The purpose of this report is to examine the history of the building now known as Allenbrook and its contextual surroundings. This analysis attempts to determine who built Allenbrook and when, as well as who lived in it before 1931, when the family of Barnett Allen Bell purchased the property and named it Allenbrook.

Roswell and the Roswell Mills – 1835 to 1852

When Roswell King, Sr. actually moved to north Georgia is uncertain. He passed through the area around 1830 on a business trip for the Bank of Darien to investigate the prospects of gold mining and the feasibility of establishing a branch bank there. By 1833, he reportedly resided in Auraria, a gold-mining town in Lumpkin County where the Bank of Darien established a branch bank. King served as cashier of the bank and sat on the Board of Directors.[7] In addition, he apparently had an interest in a gold mining concern in Lumpkin County. However, his wife never moved from the coastal town of Darien.[8] She died and was buried there in 1839, so it is unclear how permanent was King's residence in Darien.

The Georgia State Legislature officially organized Cobb County from the larger Cherokee County in 1832. Surveyors for the state ran section, district, and land lot lines throughout the county in preparation for the sixth Georgia State land lottery. Lots in the Roswell area were forty acres each, and the grant fee was $18 per lot. After the lottery, Roswell King bought land lots along Vickery Creek from those who won them. About 1836, members of the family of Roswell King moved to Cobb County. Although some historians state that Roswell King also moved to the area at this time, it is unlikely that he did so permanently before the death of his wife in Darien in 1839.

The Kings persuaded several other families from Darien to build homes in the north Georgia area as well.[9] Those who moved to Cobb County from the Roswell King family included his sons, Ralph and Barrington, and his widowed daughter, Eliza Hand, for whom Roswell King built the first permanent residence in the village, Primrose Cottage. The Kings also brought slaves numbering between thirty and forty with them.[10]

5. See Ernest DeVane and Clarece Martin, *Roswell – Historic Homes and Landmarks, A Collection of Drawings*, Roswell, GA: The Roswell Historical Society, Inc., 1974, n.p., Walsh, pp. 44-46, and James L. Skinner III, ed., *The Autobiography of Henry Merrell: Industrial Missionary to the South*, Athens, GA: University of Georgia Press, 1991, p. 463, for instance.

6. Alice Richards, "Barnett A. Bells Preserve Charm of Circa 1830 Home," Atlanta: *Constitution*, December 29, 1957. Copy found in the Roswell Historical Society Archives, Roswell, Georgia.

7. Karen Wood, *An Archeological Survey of the Presumed Location of the First Roswell Factory*, Athens, GA: Southeastern Archeological Services, Inc., 1989, p. 6.

8. Walsh, p. 240.

9. Wood, p. 6.

The original purpose of "The Colony" at Roswell was as a summer resort, away from the "sickly seasons" of lower Georgia.[11] However, the Kings immediately began to exploit the industrial potential of the waterpower afforded by Vickery Creek (now called Big Creek) as it rushed to join the Chattahoochee River. Historian Richard Coleman described the early activities of Roswell and Barrington King in "A Short History of the Roswell Manufacturing Company." Using slave labor, they first constructed a road down the slope to Vickery Creek from the bluff. They built a dam thirty feet high of cedar logs, rocks, and mud. They constructed a sawmill and, using the dam as waterpower, they "began cutting beams and planks for their first houses."[12] They also built a brick kiln, which continued to operate nearly into the twentieth century. With the timber from their sawmill and bricks from the brick kiln, they constructed a cotton mill on the northwest bank of Vickery Creek in 1839. They located this first mill three-quarters of a mile upstream of the mouth of the creek.[13] The Georgia State Legislature approved the incorporation of the mills as the Roswell Manufacturing Company in December of 1839.

Although Roswell King founded Roswell, Georgia, his son, Barrington, established the industrial base that made it a viable community. Barrington King engaged the first Superintendent for the Roswell Manufacturing Company in 1838, before construction of the mill was complete.[14] He was Henry Merrell, a northern textile engineer and operator, who arrived in Cobb County in May of 1839.[15] Merrell's responsibility was to keep the mill running smoothly by maintaining the mill machinery and overseeing the mill operators. His salary, in that first year, was $1,000 and board.

10. According to the *Sixth Census of the United States, 1840 Population Schedules, Cobb County, GA*, reviewed online at Ancestry.com, Roswell and Barrington King owned between them thirty slaves in 1840. It is unknown how many they acquired after settling at Roswell. Richard G. Coleman, "A Short History of the Roswell Manufacturing Company of Roswell, Georgia, Home of 'Roswell Grey'," unpublished manuscript in the Chattahoochee River National Recreation Area Superintendent's Office files, p. 2, states that they owned more than 40 slaves when they came to north Georgia.
11. Skinner, p. 141.
12. Coleman, p. 2.
13. Wood, p. 2.
14. Skinner, p. 140.
15. Wood, p. 7.

Although several sources assert that the Kings built Allenbrook as a residence for a superintendent of the mills, it does not appear that Merrell occupied the building. It is more likely that he lived in a boarding house or in "The Bricks," buildings constructed as apartment houses for workers at the mill. In his memoirs, Merrell mentioned that he went to the door of the company storekeeper, Mr. Fraser, one night to get a light for his candle.[16] Merrell's candle had gone out, and he could not find his matches. Merrell's use of the phrase, "...I went to his door," rather than stating that he went to the house of Mr. Fraser, probably indicates that they lived in the same building. Allenbrook is more than a mile from the early mill structures. It is unlikely that the mill superintendent lived so far from his work, especially since he conducted his business on foot. Describing the route his daily tasks took, Merrell says,

> One had to be considerable of a goat to get about that business place. At that time it was very rocky, & [sic] from the lower room of the [cotton] Factory to the upper room of the new store, and from thence round by the gin to the Wool Factory...was the means of wearing out a great many pairs of shoes for me.[17]

These buildings, the cotton factory, the store, the gin, and the wool factory, as well as the housing for the mill workers, were located within the bend of Vickery Creek immediately to the east of the village of Roswell.

It is necessary to consider whether Roswell or Barrington King built Allenbrook as a residence for Henry Merrell, as past historians have suggested. There is no documentary or circumstantial evidence for this. Henry Merrell married Elizabeth Pye Magill, a sister of the wife of Archibald Smith, in 1841. In his memoirs, Merrell never mentioned where they lived when he spoke of "setting up housekeeping." Merrell's own description of his relationship with Roswell King indicates that it is unlikely King constructed a residence for him. Merrell said that Roswell King "was not my friend...."[18] It appears neither held the other in high regard, though Merrell applauded Roswell King's energy. Barrington King apparently appreciated Merrell's efforts more. He made a gift to Merrell,

16. Skinner, p. 160.
17. Ibid., p. 164.
18. Ibid., p. 167.

possibly on the occasion of Merrell's marriage, of a building lot. However, upon leaving the employ of the Roswell Manufacturing Company, Merrell returned it to him unimproved "at the nominal price of $100.00."[19] This set of circumstances indicates that it is also improbable that Barrington King built Allenbrook for Henry Merrill's use.

James Skinner III, who compiled the autobiography of Henry Merrell from Merrell's own manuscripts, stated that Allenbrook was built about 1846 "as a residence or office...."[20] It is possible that the 1846 date is a typographical error, as he continued by saying that the Kings intended it for the use of the superintendent of the Ivy Woolen Mill, which, if built in 1846, cannot be the case since the Ivy Mill was not built until 1856. It is possible, though unlikely, that a member of the King family constructed Allenbrook for the use of some functionary of the Roswell Manufacturing Company, if not for Henry Merrell. In his memoirs, Merrell named some of those who served under him and after him.

The first overseers hired by Merrell were Enos Parker (or Eric Parker – Merrell used both names) and William Smith from the Oneida Factory in Whitesboro, New York. Unfortunately, William Smith died almost immediately upon arriving at Roswell, and Parker died not long afterward. Next, Merrell employed a Mr. Cheever, whom his friends in the North recommended. Cheever, according to Henry Merrell, "had not one practical or practicable bone in his body."[21] Merrell fired Cheever after he accidentally set the mill on fire. Because of an inability to keep Superintendents long, for whatever reason, Henry Merrell found his duties expanding to fill the void. He frequently mentioned in his memoirs that he overworked himself in the service of the Roswell Manufacturing Company. As with Henry Merrell, the likelihood that these superintendents of the cotton mill lived at Allenbrook is remote considering the distance of more than a mile between the house and the factories.

Roswell King died in 1844, and Barrington King continued to expand the holdings of the Roswell Manufacturing Company. However, Henry Merrell

commented that the original factory "found itself growing old, and plodding on in the old way with profits yearly becoming less in spite of hard work & increasing economy."[22] In the meantime, Merrell became increasingly discontent with his lot at the Roswell Manufacturing Company. In 1844, his salary was the same as that which he received in 1840, although the company shareholders upgraded his title from Superintendent to Assistant Agent that year.[23] Merrell "finally saw that there was no hope of permanent promotion to the Agency, or even...the position of Asst. Agent. There were too many Cadets of the wealthy families coming forward who would be likely to fill the office...."[24] In April of 1844, the shareholders of the Roswell Manufacturing Company allowed Henry Merrell to purchase one share of capital stock in the company for $750.[25] While attending the shareholder's meeting in October of that year, he made a motion to declare a twenty- two percent dividend on shares of stock in 1844, which motion passed.[26] It may be no coincidence that, in December of 1844, after the stock dividend distribution, Henry Merrell purchased the "Mars Hill" factory in Clarke County, Georgia, about seven miles from Athens, and moved out of Roswell permanently.

Henry Merrell left the employ of the Roswell Manufacturing Company in January of 1845. The company did not fill his position again until April of 1849 when the shareholders appointed George H. Camp as Assistant Agent.[27] Camp, a cousin of Henry Merrell, originally came to Roswell at Merrell's request to serve as the storekeeper for the Roswell Manufacturing Company store.[28] Camp did not reside at Allenbrook, either. The 1850 census of Cobb County enumerated G. H. Camp and his wife, Jane, in the home of Barrington King.[29]

19. Ibid.
20. Ibid., p. 463.
21. Skinner, p. 165.

22. Ibid., p. 173.
23. Ibid., p. 167, and "Meetings of the Stockholders of the Roswell Manufacturing Company, Roswell, Cobb County, Georgia, 1840-1900," unpublished set of original, handwritten meeting minutes, Roswell Manufacturing Company Minutes Collection, DeKalb History Center Archives, DeKalb, County, GA, p. 8. Used by permission of the DeKalb History Center.
24. Skinner, p. 181.
25. "Meetings," p. 8.
26. Ibid., p. 10.
27. Ibid., p. 21.
28. Skinner, p. 161.
29. Seventh Census of the United States, 1850 Population Schedules, Cobb County, GA, reviewed online at Ancestry.com, 2004.

Construction of Allenbrook: 1851-1856

The reason that an identifiable resident of the building now called Allenbrook cannot be found before the 1860 census is probably that it was not built until the flurry of construction activity associated with the building of the Ivy Mill in 1856. There are strong indications that building construction coincided with the establishment of the Ivy Mill by James and Thomas King. James Roswell King, son of Barrington King, listed his occupation in the 1850 census as "machinist," the result of a sojourn in Patterson, New Jersey, where he spent time learning the textile manufacturing business.[30] It appears that, in 1852, he began to put his education into practice. He purchased land at the mouth of Vickery Creek from his father for the purposes of building a mill. Although the deed does not specifically mention a mill, it states that, if James King built a dam on Vickery Creek, it must be low enough to not back up water to the factory on land lot 416.[31] This appears to indicate an intention to build a mill at the mouth of Vickery Creek.

There is some confusion among past historians about the date of construction of the Ivy Mill. Partly, this is because, in 1852, the same year that James R. King purchased land to build the Ivy Mill, the Roswell Manufacturing Company built a second cotton mill, called the New Mill. To raise the money for this construction, the Roswell Manufacturing Company apparently sought new stockholders, and James R. King was among the stockholders of the New Mill. In addition, the Roswell Manufacturing Company had a wool mill in operation in 1852 that was neither the New Mill nor the Ivy Mill. Although Wood, and later Walsh, identify it as the Ivy Mill, the wool mill cited in George White's 1854 edition of *Historical Collections of Georgia*[32] was actually the Roswell Manufacturing Company's planned new sawmill converted to a woolen mill. Cobb County Deed Book N, p. 59, dated May 18, 1843, records a transaction between B. King, N. A.

Pratt, Eliza B. Hand, and the Roswell Manufacturing Company for water and building privileges for a saw mill on lot 416.[33] However, the sawmill, if it ever did function as one, quickly became a woolen factory. Another Cobb County deed recorded a transaction between Barrington King et al. and the Roswell Manufacturing Company on October 18, 1852, for portions of land lots 415, 416, and 422. It stated: "...*also title from us in May 1843 for water privileges to saw mill, now woolen factory....*"[34] By 1855, this woolen factory was likely not even in operation, and the meeting minutes of the Roswell Manufacturing Company shareholders cease to mention wool production.

In 1855, the shareholders of the Roswell Manufacturing Company appointed a committee to evaluate the machinery at this wool factory and sell it.[35] The committee estimated the total value of the wool production machinery to be $300 and authorized the company's Agent, George H. Camp, to sell it at that price. In 1856, James King built his mill, and, after his brother, Thomas, became a partner, they named the factory the Ivy Mill.[36] James R. King bought the wool manufacturing machinery from the earlier wool plant in April of 1857 for $711.54 and installed it in the Ivy Mill, which apparently went into operation shortly thereafter.

Previous writers and historians have advanced various theories regarding the occupants of Allenbrook in its early days. These theories include a superintendent of the Roswell Mills, a superintendent of the Ivy Mill (often said to be Theophile Roché or Samuel Bonfoy or Bonfoir), the bookkeeper of the Ivy Mill (also said to be Mr. Bonfoy), and, during the Civil War, loom boss, John N. Brown. Oddly, it appears that no previous writer has considered the possibility that it was built for and occupied by the owner of the Ivy Mill, James R. King. It is useful to consider the likelihood of as many of these scenarios as possible.

The Federal census records provide clues regarding the tenant of Allenbrook in 1860. It does not appear that the family of George H. Camp, superintendent of the Roswell Mills, occupied it. The census enumerated the Camp family before Hugh W.

30. Ibid., and Skinner, p. 168.
31. Chad O. Braley, Karen G. Wood, and T. Jeffrey Price, *An Archeological and Historical Survey of a Fifteen Acre Tract in Roswell, Fulton County, Georgia*, Athens, GA: Southeastern Archeological Services, Inc., 1992, p. 11.
32. Walsh, p. 42.
33. Braley, Wood, and Price, p. 11.
34. Ibid.
35. "Meetings," p. 46.
36. Braley, Wood, and Price, p. 12.

Proudfoot.[37] According to a current map of the Roswell Historic District, the home of Hugh Proudfoot is at the north end of the Roswell Historic District, whereas Allenbrook is on the south end. The home of Barrington King is between the two. The census, therefore, indicates that the Camp family lived north of Hugh Proudfoot rather than south of Barrington King. However, the census records do reveal possible residents of Allenbrook. Enumerated immediately after the family of Barrington King, whose occupation is listed as President of the Roswell Manufacturing Company, is the family of A. Vanzant, of Delaware, listed as Superintendent of the Roswell Manufacturing Company. Comparing this to the map of the Roswell Historic District, it appears that Allenbrook could have been the next house to be enumerated if the census-taker went south from that of Barrington King, located south of the town square in Roswell. It is logical to conclude that the tenant of Allenbrook in 1860 could have been A. Vanzant with his wife and three daughters. Also living with them was one son, John J. Vanzant, Overseer at the Roswell Manufacturing Company, with his wife, one son, and two daughters. Although the 1860 census lists several other overseers for the Roswell Manufacturing Company, as well as lesser functionaries such as loom bosses and watchmen, A. Vanzant is the only Superintendent listed. If the Vanzants were the residents of Allenbrook, it might explain the legend that a member of the King family built Allenbrook as a residence for a manager of a mill.

John N. Brown, overseer for the Roswell Manufacturing Company, is listed immediately after Vanzant. However, he and his wife, Mary, along with their three children, were boarders in the household of a factory hand, Susan White, with her six children. This enumeration provides an interesting insight into the conditions in which the factory workers lived. If these factory workers lived at Allenbrook, two families with a total of nine children were living in a house consisting of four rooms plus an upstairs loft. However, it is unlikely that either Vanzant or the White/Brown household lived at Allenbrook in 1860 as all of the working members of these households are enumerated as employees of the Roswell Manufacturing Company

cotton mill more than a mile away. Where Samuel Bonfoy/Bonfoir lived could not be ascertained from records available for this research.

However, there is a stronger candidate for tenancy at Allenbrook. That candidate is James R. King himself, with his wife, Francis, three sons, and one daughter. Although enumerated in the 1850 census as a "machinist" and included in the household of his father, the 1860 census listed him as a "Woollen Mfcture," [sic] indicating his status as an owner of the Ivy Mill. He married Elizabeth Frances Prince about 1851. This marriage most likely prompted construction of a home for the newlyweds, a common occurrence in their society. The 1860 census enumerates James King and family after a long list of mill workers and other laborers. There are ninety households enumerated between James R. King and his father. It is probable that the census-taker worked his way around the mill area on "Factory Hill" in Roswell before proceeding south toward the Chattahoochee River and, thus, to Allenbrook. Another clue that James King built Allenbrook and lived in it for a time is the substantial nature of the construction. It is by far the largest house of the period in that area, with functional and decorative features beyond any built for mill workers in Roswell before or since. For instance, "The Bricks," built by Roswell King for his workers, though also constructed of brick, housed more than four families in one building. The apartments in "The Bricks" consisted of two small rooms downstairs and one room upstairs, with a narrow stairway connecting them. Allenbrook, apparently built originally for a single family, contained four ample rooms downstairs with an open loft upstairs. A fireplace with a decorative mantel provided warmth to each downstairs room.

The construction and detailing of Allenbrook indicates that the builder intended it to house someone of more status than a mill employee had in those times. A third clue that James R. King and family lived close to the Ivy Mill is that, unlike workers living near his father, Barrington King, who were listed as factory hands, the census listed those living near James King as woolen mill workers. Located uphill from the site of the Ivy Mill, but within walking distance of it, Allenbrook is the logical place for the superintendent of the mill to live. It appears from the census records that the only superintendent of the woolen mill in 1860 was James

---

37. *Eighth Census of the United States, 1860 Population Schedule, Cobb County, GA*, reviewed online at Ancestry.com, 2004.

Roswell King. Thomas King, who owned the land on which Allenbrook stands with his brother, does not appear in the 1860 Cobb County, Georgia Federal census records. Neither Mr. Bonfoy, reportedly the bookkeeper for the Ivy Mill, nor Theophile Rochè, the legendary Overseer of the mill, both proposed as tenants at Allenbrook, appear in the census records of 1860.

The Civil War Years: 1861-1865

Shortly after the Civil War began, the Ivy Mill contracted to make cloth for the Confederate government. The mill manufactured a particular cloth for uniforms known as "Roswell Grey," a wool- cotton blend that did not shrink and was warmer than flannel. The cotton mills of the Roswell Manufacturing Company produced cotton sheeting, thread, rope, and other woven cotton products and sold them to the Confederate government as well as to clients outside the region. This production had serious consequences for the mills and the mill workers later in the war.

Barrington King and three of his sons enlisted in the Confederate Army at the outbreak of the Civil War.[38] One son, Barrington Simerall King, enlisted in Cobb's Legion, eventually attaining the rank of Lieutenant Colonel. Clifford A. King, the youngest of the King sons, served as a Cadet in Georgia's Infantry, Third Battalion. Thomas E. King enlisted and was elected Captain of Company H, Seventh Infantry Regiment, Georgia, organized in May of 1861 at Atlanta.[39] This regiment, assigned to the Army of Northern Virginia, went almost immediately into battle. James King remained in Roswell to oversee the management of Ivy Mill. It is very likely that A. Vanzant left Georgia at the outbreak of the war. Originally from Delaware and a newcomer to the area, he likely returned to the northern states after hostilities commenced. The

rosters of local militia units of the Confederate Army do not list his name. On July 21, 1861, Thomas King was severely wounded in the leg at the first Battle of Bull Run.[40] He returned home to Roswell to recuperate.[41] June 28, 1863 saw the organization of the "Roswell Battalion," Company C of the Georgia Cavalry. Captain James R. King and Captain Thomas E. King, among others, led the battalion. Joseph H. King and Ralph B. King, Sr., also sons of Barrington King, served as First Lieutenants. The stated purpose of this battalion was "for home defense to protect the portion of the state of Georgia lying north of Atlanta to the Alabama and Tennessee lines...not to be called upon except to repel a raid of the Yankees and not to be kept on service longer than is necessary for that special purpose."[42] In addition, the organizing charter stipulated that "a large portion [of the force is] composed of detailed men now at work for the Confederate State Government under Major G. W. Cunningham, Q. M. for Atlanta at Roswell Factories, 20 miles north of Atlanta. It is composed of men and boys from 60 years down to 16 years of age." In accordance with an agreement between the officers of the Roswell Manufacturing Company and the Confederate Government, a unit of the Confederate Army worked in the Roswell Mills.[43] This battalion remained inactive until the following year when the Federal forces entered Georgia. A comparison of the roster with the 1860 census reveals many surnames in the roster of the Roswell Battalion found earlier enumerated as factory hands in the 1860 census. Thomas King left the Roswell Battalion in September of 1863 and joined the Army of Tennessee under General Bragg. On September 19, 1863, General Preston invited King to serve as his staff aide. Heavy fighting engulfed Thomas King at the Battle of Chickamauga, and he was killed there.

In the spring of 1864, Union troops invaded Georgia, heading toward Atlanta under the direction of General William Tecumseh Sherman. General Sherman planned to destroy every mill and factory aiding the Confederacy that stood in his

38. Tammy H. Galloway, ed., *Dear Old Roswell – Civil War Letters of the King Family of Roswell, Georgia*, Macon, GA: Mercer University Press, 2003, p. 5 and Coleman, pp. 5-6.

39. Galloway, p. 5, and "CO. H, 7th Infantry Regiment, Volunteers, Army of Northern Virginia, Confederate States of America, Cobb County, Georgia, 'Roswell Guards,' " posted with a brief history of the Company at <www.geocities.com/jshop24jhawkins/ RoswellGuards.html>, reviewed online, 2004.

40. Galloway, pp. 5-6.
41. Walsh, p. 72.
42. "Georgia Cavalry Local Defense Troops, Co. A, B, & C Cavalry Battalion, Georgia Cavalry, Volunteers, Army of Tennessee, Confederate States of America, Cobb County, Georgia, 'Roswell Battalion,' " posted with a brief history of the Company at <www.geocities,com/ jshop27jhawkins/RoswellBattallion.html>, reviewed online, 2004.
43. "Meetings," pp. 79-80.

way, including cotton, woolen, and grist mills, and all iron manufacturers. The Roswell Manufacturing Company's collection of cotton, wool, and flour mills made it a worthy target.

Two weeks before Union forces arrived in Roswell, Barrington King took the books for the Roswell Manufacturing Company and Ivy Mill to Savannah, where his oldest son, the Rev. Charles King, lived.[44] Other wealthy families from Roswell also sought refuge in Atlanta, Macon, Augusta, or Savannah. James King remained in Roswell. As Captain of the Roswell Battalion, he was under orders to retreat south of the Chattahoochee River and burn the bridge should the Federal forces advance as far as Roswell. Before he left, he instructed his "head man" and the operatives to remain at their posts in the mill or in their homes until driven out by the soldiers.[45] Although Hitt identifies this "head man" as Samuel Bonfoy, several other sources identify him as a French weaver employed at the mill, Theophile Rochè. Rochè arrived in Roswell in 1863, seeking work.[46] He was initially employed at the cotton mill, but quickly moved to the woolen mill. Although the circumstances are not clear, it appears that an arrangement was made between James King and Rochè, in which King consigned an interest in the mill to his weaver, the Frenchman, Theophile Rochè. The intention was to make it appear that a citizen of a foreign, neutral power owned and operated the mill. Both France and Great Britain declared neutrality in the conflict. Therefore, to fire upon the property of a citizen of a neutral power could be considered an act of war against the neutral country, a thing to be avoided while the United States was already engaged in its own, internal war. However, this stricture did not apply if the citizen engaged in activities supporting the rebellion.

"As Union troops advanced on Roswell on July 6, 1864, Rochè hoisted a French flag in an effort to save the mills."[47] When the troops arrived at the mills, "Captain Joseph G. Vale, Company M, Seventh Pennsylvania Cavalry, was told by British and French employees that the mills should not be harmed because they operated under a neutral flag."[48] According to Captain Joseph G. Vale, of Company M, Seventh Pennsylvania Cavalry, the following day, General Kenner Garrard "stepped into the factory and passing through, found the operators busy engaged in making heavy cotton cloth, and a very little investigation showed that on each Webb, of piece, the cabalistic letters, C.S.A., were woven in the wool."[49] This eyewitness account has led some historians to associate Theophile Rochè with the Roswell Manufacturing Company cotton mills and other historians and writers to associate him with the Ivy wool mill. Vale continues by saying that the attention of the supposedly "neutral" subjects of Great Britain and France was directed to this problematic production. They were instructed to remove the French flag that was flying on the flagpole, surrender their money and papers to the military authorities, and "notify all the operators to leave the building at once."[50] When they refused to comply, the building was evacuated by force, the books and papers of the company were seized, placed under guard, and forwarded to army headquarters, and the buildings were burned "with their contents, machinery and stock on hand, thoroughly destroyed."[51] This total destruction seems to indicate the activities at the cotton mill buildings, but Garrard's report to Sherman specified that the French flag flew over the woolen mill.[52] It does not mention any other flags but specifically noted that the United States flag was not flying. However, Rochè was later given a receipt for two French flags, and an investigation by the French and American Claims Commission in 1882 revealed that a French flag also flew over Bulloch Hall.[53]

At the cotton mills, soldiers impressed large amounts of cloth, thread, and rope for use by the Union Army, and then set the buildings on fire, destroying them. At the Ivy Mill, they dumped the machinery into the river and started a small fire. However, the fire did not severely damage the mill.[54] In fact, enough flooring remained in the Ivy

44. "Meetings,". p. 85.
45. James King, quoted in Hitt, p. 3.
46. *Boston Post,* anonymous correspondent, n.d. A copy and a transcript of this article are housed in the Archives of the Roswell Historical Society.
47. DeVane and Martin, n.p.
48. Braley, Wood, and Price, p. 16.
49. Captain Joseph G. Vale, *Minty and the Cavalry,* Edwin K. Meyer, Printer and Binder, 1886, quoted in Hitt, p. 14.
50. Ibid.
51. Ibid.
52. General Kenner Garrard to Major General William Tecumseh Sherman, quoted in Hitt, p. 20.
53. T. D. Adams, sworn statement to the French and American Claims Commission, October 31, 1882, n.p. A transcript of this statement is housed in the Archives of the Roswell Historical Society.

Mill to enable General Dodge, following on the heels of General Garrard two days later, to construct a bridge over the Chattahoochee to replace the one burned by the retreating Confederate forces.

The Union soldiers destroyed fifteen mill structures, but, according to Barrington King, did little harm to most of the homes of the citizens of Roswell.[55] General Sherman ordered that the owners, supervisors and workers at the mills be arrested and charge with treason.[56] Of course, most of the shareholders had already left town, and the soldiers did not arrest the remaining shareholder, the Reverend Nathaniel Pratt. The army forced the arrested workers, primarily women with their children, to walk to Marietta and then put them on trains heading north to Chattanooga, Tennessee. From there, they were sent to places such as Nashville, Tennessee, Louisville, Kentucky, and Jeffersonville, Indiana. Sherman also gave his approval for the troops to hang Rochè for his attempt at deceit if they so desired, but they spared his life. DeVane and Martin, likely quoting other sources, assert that "he was arrested for treason and sent north for the duration of the war."[57] However, T. D. Adams, testifying for the French and American Claims Commission in 1882 asserts that Rochè was never arrested, although he accompanied the mill workers to Marietta three days after the Union soldiers captured Roswell.[58] He also apparently went part of the way north with them. Rochè left the trainload of mill workers somewhere between Chattanooga and Nashville. He traveled to New York City and, from there, returned to France.[59] Adams stated that he saw Rochè in New York City in October, 1864. Rochè told Adams that he had in his possession a large amount of Confederate bonds and currency belonging to the widow of Thomas E. King, which he intended to dispose for her.[60] However, Adams noted that a conversation with Mrs. King about 1878 revealed that she never heard

from Rochè again and never received anything for the funds with which she entrusted him.

There is conflicting information regarding the tenant at Allenbrook during the Civil War. Three candidates emerge. James Roswell King probably continued to live there with his family until some time in 1864, before the occupation of Roswell by the Federal army. There is no actual evidence that he moved between the 1860 census and the end of the war. The census does not indicate any superintendent of the Ivy Mill, so James King likely functioned in that capacity in his mill. Allenbrook is appropriately located to be a residence for an employee at the Ivy Mill, though likely too far from the cotton mills to house one of the cotton mill workers. It is probable that King sent his wife and family out of Roswell along with most of the other wealthy families of the town before he left for Atlanta with his troops. This would have left Allenbrook empty if not occupied by someone else. It appears that the wealthy families of the south hired others to occupy their houses and be responsible for their safekeeping when the owners themselves left for safer locations. For instance, William King, in Marietta, wrote in his diary that he could not remain there much longer but felt certain that to leave his house unprotected would "secure its destruction."[61] He was more concerned about roving bands of Confederate soldiers than he was about depredations from the occupying Union forces. He hoped to get Mr. Rowland and his family from Roswell to occupy his house in Marietta, but restrictions on travel between the two towns by civilians made this impossible. It is likely, then, that other member of the King family might have hired others to occupy their homes for security while the owners went to safer quarters. The question is who might have occupied Allenbrook after the James King family left Roswell.

According to both Hitt and Walsh, John Brown, loom boss, with his wife, Mary, occupied it during the War Between the States.[62] However, neither author provides any real evidence for this assertion. Walsh's book, *Roswell - A Pictorial History*, includes a map of the Roswell area reproduced from *The Official Atlas of the Civil War* (author and publisher not given) that shows a structure in the approximate location of Allenbrook, labeled "Brown." However,

---

54. Galloway, p. 8.
55. "Meetings," pp. 85-87.
56. Gail D'Avino, preparer, *Assessment of No Adverse Effect to Allenbrook, the Robertson House, the H. S. Weaver House, the Roswell Historic National Register District and Ivy/Laurel Mill (Site 9FU228)*, Atlanta: Fulton County Government, 1997, p. 7.
57. DeVane and Martin, n.p.
58. Adams, n.p.
59. Hitt, p. 156.
60. Adams, n.p.

61. William King, quoted in Hitt, p. 125.
62. Walsh, pp. 53, 173.

the map also labels the Ivy Mill as "Joy Mill" and contains several other misspellings and incorrect labeling, so the validity of the information on this map is questionable. Nevertheless, it is possible that the John Brown family occupied Allenbrook for James King briefly before the capture of Roswell by Union forces. The 1860 Federal Census for Cobb County listed two J. Browns, both with wives whose names begin with the letter "M." J. N. Brown, enumerated in the household of Susan White, located next to the residence of A. Vanzant, Superintendent of the Roswell Manufacturing Company, gave his occupation as Overseer with the Roswell Manufacturing Company. The other, J. C. Brown, listed his occupation as Watchman for the Roswell Manufacturing Company. J. C. Brown, however, owned his own home, so he would not be living at Allenbrook, owned by James and Thomas King. Neither of these J. Browns appears to be living close to the Ivy Mill, based on their location in the census records. The roster of the Roswell Battalion of 1863 lists three John Browns: John C. Brown and John J. Brown, both Privates, as well as John N. Brown, Sergeant. It is possible that James King moved his family to Barrington Hall, the home of his father, or to some other location in Roswell after the 1860 census.

After his brother, Thomas, died at Chickamauga, Thomas King's widow moved to Bulloch Hall with her children. James King might have moved his family there to act as her protector. This would have caused King to be living relatively far from the mill he owned and superintended. However, it would leave Allenbrook available for residence by John and Mary Brown as asserted by Walsh and Hitt. As members of the Roswell Battalion, John J. Brown and John C. Brown probably left Roswell when Captain James King retreated with his men to Atlanta. John N. Brown, loom boss, remained in Roswell and continued to run the mill. He, with his wife, Mary, were arrested and sent to Louisville, and, from there, to Indianapolis, Indiana, and so left Allenbrook, if they were indeed living there, behind.[63] Real evidence that they lived there, however, remains elusive. The most popular, and least likely, candidate to be a tenant at Allenbrook is Theophile Rochè. Several writers, DeVane and Martin as well as Skinner, for instance, suggest that Rochè used Allenbrook as both a residence and an office. Given the popularity of this theory, it is useful here to consider why this scenario is unlikely.

Theophile Rochè did not appear in the 1860 Federal Census of Cobb County or in any other 1860 United States censuses. However, beginning in 1863, he worked as a weaver for the Ivy Woolen Mill, though he first worked as a weaver for the Roswell Manufacturing Company cotton mill. Theophile Rochè is likely the person listed as "Theodore" Rochè in the 1863 roster of the Roswell Battalion. This indicates that he resided in Roswell by June of that year. Nevertheless, they left him behind a year later when the Roswell Battalion headed for Atlanta. Although Rochè claimed he was an owner of the Ivy Mill, no documentary evidence for this claim has been uncovered. Theophile Rochè filed a claim for damages with the French and American Claims Commission in 1883, but the Commission dismissed the claim for lack of prosecution.[64] This may be because Rochè again lived in France at the time, or it also may be because he did not have sufficient proof of his ownership to prosecute his claim. T. D. Adams, in his statement to the Claims Commission commented that that "Roche was not possessed of any means."[65] Although James King later testified that he left the mill under the charge of his "head man" when he pulled his battalion south across the Chattahoochee, it is probable that this title, if he meant Roche, was quite recent. Author Michael Hitt names Samuel Bonfoy/Bonfoir as the superintendent of the Ivy Mill. Bonfoy/Bonfoir was arrested with the other mill worker when Union forces came through Roswell. Theophile Rochè was likely a "superintendent" for only about four days before he left Roswell for Marietta with the other mill workers. It is apparent that James King based Theophile Rochè's elevation from weaver to superintendent of the Ivy Mill solely on Rochè's French citizenship, hoping to protect his mill from the approaching Federal forces. This citizenship only assumed importance as the advance of the enemy became certain. Therefore, it is improbable that Rochè functioned as superintendent before James R. King left Roswell, making it extremely unlikely that he ever inhabited Allenbrook on any kind of a permanent basis. In fact, evidence from T. D. Adams reveals that, when the Union forces took Roswell, Rochè was staying at Bulloch Hall. He had apparently been entrusted with its safekeeping by

---

63. Hitt, p. 156.

64. DeVane and Martin, n.p.
65. Adams, n.p.

Mrs. Thomas E. King when she left Roswell on July 5 for safer quarters. To preserve his charge, he also raised the French flag above this residence.[66] Fortunately, the Federal soldiers were instructed to destroy only the manufacturing concerns and to protect the homes of citizens, so this action did not have the same deleterious effect on Bulloch Hall that it had on Ivy Mill.[67]

Other mill superintendents also remained in Roswell; Rochè's presence was not unique. According to Walsh, the silver communion service of the Presbyterian Church came into the possession of Olney Eldredge, mill superintendent, during the occupation of Roswell by the first wave of Federal troops. Members of the congregation transported the communion service to the home of Eldredge hidden in a barrel of oats.[68] From there, it was apparently carried, piece by piece in baskets of food, to an elderly, infirm woman, Mrs. Stephen Whitmire, who was likely allowed to remain in Roswell when the rest of the mill workers, including the daughter who brought her the baskets of food, were sent to Marietta.[69] Eldredge and Mr. Bonfoir, were arrested with the other workers and removed to Marietta.[70] Eldredge, at least, returned to Roswell by the end of the year. T. D. Adams, Clerk for the Roswell Manufacturing Company and assistant Postmaster of Roswell during the Civil War, also remained behind, but he was never arrested and remained in Roswell until August, 1864.[71] After the initial detail of Union soldiers left Roswell, it appears that other families moved into some of the great houses in town, if they were not employed to reside in them before. The Reverend Nathaniel Pratt, writing to Barrington Simerall King in December of 1864, detailed the damage to the houses of Barrington King, the Dunwoodys, the Mintons, the Proudfoots, and the Smiths, as well as to that of James King. Most of the damage was done not by Union forces but by Confederate soldiers home on leave, with or without permission. He commented that "the families living in them do not keep them very neatly."[72] It is not known who these families were at the time; certainly Theophile Rochè was no longer at Bulloch Hall, and John and Mary Brown were no longer at Allenbrook. Barrington Simmerall King, son of Barrington King, accompanied his wife and children to Roswell the following month and installed them at Barrington Hall.[73] By then, Roswell was almost a ghost town, with only the old and infirm remaining, along with a few who were not obviously associated with the Roswell mills, such as the Rev. Pratt and T. D. Adams.

On reflection, one can hardly fault those left behind for making use of the available resources in a time of deep privation. The paternalistic members of the wealthy class abandoned them to the tender mercies of the Union army and headed for safer ground. Thanks to the "liberal foraging on the countryside" of soldiers from both sides of the conflict, starvation was a very real possibility. Even firewood for cooking became scarce as soldiers demolished fences and small wooden structures for use in their own campfires. It is a small wonder that the remaining population felt no great sense of responsibility to the absentee owners of the properties they occupied.

Reconstruction and Change: 1866-1932

The war lasted less than a year after the burning of the Roswell Mills. Barrington King returned to Roswell in June of 1865 and began to rebuild the second cotton mill, called the New Mill. However, he died in 1866, in the middle of his rebuilding project, and his holdings passed to his widow, his surviving children, and the widows of his sons who did not survive him.[74] The shareholders of the Roswell Manufacturing Company elected George H. Camp as President of the company. He continued to rebuild the New Mill according to the plans of Barrington King and presented it to them completed at the October 1867 meeting of the shareholders, along with his resignation.[75] As inducement to withdraw his resignation, the

---

66. Adams, n.p.
67. Captain Robert P. Kennedy, U.S.A to Captain d. E. Livermore, 3rd Ohio Volunteer Cavalry, U.S.A., July 6, 1864. A transcript of this order is housed in the Archives of the Roswell Historical Society.
68. Walsh, p. 66.
69. Ibid.
70. William King, quoted in Hitt, p. 50.
71. Adams, n.p.

72. Walsh, p. 67.
73. Galloway, p. 98.
74. Coleman, p. 4.
75. "Meetings," pp. 107-108.

shareholders offered to raise his pay to $5,000 per year. They also offered to buy or rent the home of James R. King for Camp, indicating that they did not expect King to want it within the next year. Camp declined their offers, and the shareholders promptly voted to offer the presidency of the company to General Andrew J. Hansell, another shareholder of the Roswell Manufacturing Company.

In fact, James R. King did not immediately return to Roswell. After the fall of Roswell, his battalion was made a permanent company by Brigadier General M. J. Wright and ordered to turn their artillery over to the arsenal in Atlanta. They were then made a mounted company, but, although they were mustered as a mounted company, many of the men never received horses. "After the fall of Atlanta, Captain King was ordered to report to General Howell Cobb, who assigned the company to General Alfred Iverson, who in turn assigned them to Hannon's brigade."[76] He was captured by Federal troops about August 28, 1864 at Macon, Georgia.[77] However, in February 1865, he visited Roswell, so he must have been released. After the war, King moved his family to New Jersey, where he remained until about 1868. While in New Jersey, he represented the Roswell Manufacturing Company in the purchase of new machinery for the rebuilding of the New Mill. When he returned to Georgia, James King did not return to Allenbrook. The 1870 census enumerated him in Marietta as an "Owner of Cotton Mills."[78] By the 1880 census, however, he again lived in Roswell.[79] According to the Historic American Buildings Survey records, James R. King purchased the estate known as Holly Hill in Roswell shortly after the Civil War,[80] so it is probable that he lived there and not at Allenbrook in 1880. When King rebuilt the Ivy Mill is not known, but "an 1880 census report on water power noted that an existing frame dam was improved in 1871, which suggests that the mill may have been rebuilt at this time."[81]

However, King had other enterprises in mind than textile production. In 1873, he revived interest in a railroad connection between Roswell and Atlanta and set to work on the grading using leased convict labor in place of the slaves used before the Civil War.[82]

James R. King bought Thomas King's share of the Ivy Mill and Allenbrook on July 16, 1874. Two weeks later, he sold his holdings to the Empire Manufacturing Company, in which he had an interest. The Empire Manufacturing Company produced cotton goods at the Ivy Mill for only a short time. In 1875, James Robertson, then president of the Roswell Manufacturing Company, undertook the task of disposing of the Empire Mills property and settling its debts. He first sold the mill and lands to the estates of Edward Houston and Charles R. Mills, apparently to clear a lien on the property. Then, the Roswell Manufacturing Company bought the property and moved the mill machinery to its new mill. In 1877, The Laurel Mills Manufacturing Company bought the property and converted it back to a wool mill.[83] Although the mills again manufactured the "Roswell Gray" material for uniforms, the mill ceased operation in 1911 when the company went into bankruptcy.[84] In June of 1917, George A. Wing [one of the partners in the Laurel Mills Manufacturing Company] sold portions of lots 456, 457, 421 and two nearby lots to I. M. Roberts et. al. The March 1, 1917 edition of the Cobb Country Times announced that the "Atlanta Woolen Mills Manufacturing Company have bought a part of the old machinery at Laurel Mills here and are moving it down there to put in operation soon."[85] The rest of the machinery was purchased by the Georgia Manufacturing Company and moved to Gainesville.[86] In 1923, Georgia Power Company purchased the Laurel Mill property, including Allenbrook.[87] At that time, Georgia Power was acquiring properties for the purpose of building hydroelectric power plants, which is likely

76. Hitt, p. 103.
77. Ibid., p. 117.
78. *Ninth Census of the United States, 1870 Population Schedule, Cobb County, GA,* reviewed online at Ancestry.com, 2004.
79. *Tenth Census of the United States, 1880 Population Schedule, Cobb County, GA,* reviewed online at Ancestry.com, 2004.
80. National Park Service. Historic American Buildings Survey/Historic American Engineering Record (HABS/ HAER). Washington, D.C.: Library of Congress Prints and Photographs Division, 1936. Reviewed online at <http://memory.loc.gov/ammem/hhtml/hhome.html>.

81. Braley, Wood, and Price, p. 17.
82. Walsh, p. 85.
83. Anonymous, "Background History," unpublished manuscript found in the archives of the Superintendent of the Chattahoochee River National Recreation Area, n.d., n.p.
84. DeVane and Martin, n.p., and Anonymous, "Background History," n.p.
85. Braley, Wood, and Price, p. 18.
86. Records of the Roswell Bank, Boxes 1-4, housed in the Archives of the Roswell Historical Society.
87. Anonymous, "Background History," n.p.

the cause of the purchase of the Laurel Mill properties. By 1924, the Georgia Power Company, as well as locals in search of building materials, were dismantling the Laurel Mill. A severe drought in 1925 caused the Georgia Power Company to abandon plans to build more hydroelectric power plants. The company never built on the Laurel Mill site. In 1926, the Directors of the Roswell Manufacturing Company used the original hewn roof and floor timbers from the abandoned buildings to enlarge their newest mill, built in 1882.[88]

An anonymous researcher documented some of the residents of Allenbrook during the time the Laurel Mills Manufacturing Company owned the property. This researcher apparently gleaned most of the information through personal interviews conducted some time in the late 1970s or early 1980s. According to this researcher, Nathaniel L. Sherman lived in Allenbrook in the late 1880s. His descendants believed that he was a superintendent or manager for the Laurel Mill.[89] The Sherman family had a long association with the King family as well as with the Ivy/Laurel Mill. Nathaniel L. Sherman's father, Randolph E. Sherman, a native of Rhode Island, appears in the 1840 Federal Census records of Cobb County after the enumeration of Willis Ball.[90] Willis Ball was the carpenter-architect whom Barrington King hired to build his home, Barrington Hall. Other Roswell friends of the Kings also hired Ball to design and build their "temple houses," the Greek Revival mansions that the wealthy residents constructed for their use in the early days of Roswell.[91] A northeastern carpenter himself, Randolph E. Sherman probably worked for Willis Ball constructing these houses. In the minutes of the 1852 fall meeting of the Roswell Manufacturing Company, Sherman's name is on a list of renters of "The Bricks," the apartment buildings reportedly built for workers at the company's cotton mill. The list included the notation, "2 yrs," indicating the length of time he had lived at "The Bricks."[92] However, this should probably not be considered an indication that Sherman worked in the cotton mill as he very likely continued to use his carpenter skills to make a living.

In the 1860 Federal census records of Cobb County, Randolph E. Sherman and his family apparently lived closer to the Ivy Mill. In fact, they lived only six houses away from James R. King and his family at the time.[93] It is possible that James and Thomas King employed Sherman as a carpenter in the construction of the Ivy Mill, especially considering his association with Roswell and Barrington King. Randolph E. Sherman's name is also on the roster of the Seventh Infantry Regiment of Georgia, of which Thomas King was captain. Sherman's three sons, John D., Nathaniel L., and Luther Sherman, enlisted as Privates in the same company. Pvt. Luther Sherman was captured and sent to military prison, first in Louisville, Kentucky, and later to Camp Douglas in Illinois, where he died.[94] It is unknown whether Randolph E. Sherman survived the conflict. He is not listed in the 1870 census of Cobb County. Nathaniel Sherman and his older brother, John, appear in this census, their families living side by side, in the Lemons District of Cobb County. Both worked in a woolen mill. By the 1880 census, both Nathaniel and John Sherman lived in Roswell again. The census-taker enumerated them living close to one another and both working in a woolen mill.[95] This mill is the Laurel Mill, the only wool mill in the area.

According to his descendants, Nathaniel Sherman lived at Allenbrook in 1887 when he purchased an adjoining property and built a house for his daughter. This house later became known as "the McDerment House."[96] It is not possible to check the 1890 census for Sherman families and McDerment families living in close proximity because fire destroyed the census records. A search of the 1900 Federal Census records inconveniently revealed two separate Sherman families living next to two separate McDerment families, making it difficult to determine which family possibly lived at Allenbrook.[97] However, a comparison of the ages of the McDerment wives in this census indicated

88. Coleman, p. 6.
89. Anonymous, "Background History," n.p.
90. *Sixth Census of the United States, 1840 Population Schedule, Cobb County, GA,* reviewed online at Ancestry.com, 2004.
91. Walsh, p. 39.
92. "Meetings," p. 35.

93. *Eighth Census of the United States, 1860 Population Schedule, Cobb County, GA,* reviewed online at Ancestry.com, 2004.
94. Hitt, pp. 140, 145.
95. *Tenth Census of the United States, 1880 Population Schedule, Cobb County, GA,* reviewed online at Ancestry.com, 2004.
96. Anonymous, "Background History," n.p.

that the most likely candidate to be a daughter of Nathaniel L. Sherman lived in the dwelling designated 149 in the census records. Unfortunately, age and bad ink obscure the names on the page, so it is not possible to compare them to the names of the children of Nathaniel L. Sherman in the 1880 census. If the McDerment family living in dwelling 149 is the daughter of Nathaniel Sherman with her husband and children, the likely residents of Allenbrook are the members of the Sherman family listed immediately before them. In 1900, this was the family of John D. Sherman, brother of Nathaniel Sherman. By 1900, John D. Sherman and his son, William, were shareholders in the Oxbo Road Manufacturing Company, also known as "The Pants Factory," in Roswell. A further clue that they lived at least near the Ivy Mill is that the census listed some of them, as well as some of their neighbors, as woolen mill workers.

Between 1903 and 1905, two families occupied the building simultaneously. The Copeland and Beaver families rented the house from the Laurel Mills Manufacturing Company. Ewell "Ollie" Copeland, who worked for the Laurel Mills, died there in 1905.[98] The residents of Allenbrook between 1905 and 1932 are unknown. However, the building was vacant for some time before 1932, when the Barnett Allen Bells purchased the property. By 1932 it, was in a state of disrepair. It is probable, therefore, that no one occupied the building from at least 1923, when the Georgia Power Company purchased the property, until 1932. It may have been empty as early as 1911, when the Laurel Mills Manufacturing Company closed its doors.

On January 1, 1932, Milton County, a small county north of Fulton County, merged with Fulton County. To facilitate this merger, Cobb County ceded a small eastern portion to Fulton County, providing a "land bridge" to the former Milton County. This political realignment gave Fulton County its unusual shape and moved the City of Roswell, as well as Allenbrook and the former Ivy Mill, out of Cobb County and into Fulton County.[99]

Barnett Allen Bell and Allenbrook: 1932-1978

Mr. and Mrs. Barnett Allen Bell purchased Allenbrook and surrounding grounds in 1932 and moved there from their home in Peachtree Heights, an unincorporated area north of Atlanta.[100] According to the 1930 Federal Census records, Barnett Allen Bell was born in Georgia about 1892, and his wife, Agnes M. Bell, was born in the Irish Free State about 1893.[101] Barnett Bell was, according to the 1930 census, an "estimator for a power company," presumably Georgia Power Company, from which they purchased their property, naming their new estate Allenbrook.[102] According to the anonymous researcher who interviewed Barnett Bell, Jr. in 1980, the house originally had only four rooms, two on either side of a wide hallway down the center, plus an attic loft accessed by a steep and narrow set of stairs without handrails. The Bells remodeled it in the 1930s, adding a bath downstairs and the two bedrooms and bath upstairs.[103]

The National Park Service acquired the house and surrounding land in 1978 from Mrs. Barnett Allen Bell, though she continued to live there until November or December of 1979.[104] The Park Service included Allenbrook in the Chattahoochee River National Recreation Area at the entrance to the Vickery Creek Unit of the Park. In 1983, the National Park Service, the Roswell Historical Society, and the City of Roswell reached an agreement that allowed the Historical Society to operate and maintain the house as their headquarters and as a welcome center for the city. While used by the Roswell Historical Society, the building housed a museum, a meeting room, a kitchen, a gift shop, and offices. In 1988, the City of Roswell expanded their Historic District to the Chattahoochee River, thus encompassing Allenbrook within its confines. The Roswell

97. *Twelfth Census of the United States, 1900, Population Schedule, Cobb County, GA,* reviewed online at Ancestry.com, 2004.
98. Anonymous, "Background History," n.p.
99. "Official Fulton County Website, Fulton County, Georgia – History," reviewed at www.co.fulton.ga.us.com.

100. Richards, n.p., and *Fifteenth Census of the United States, 1930 Population Schedule, Fulton County, GA,* reviewed online at Ancestry.com, 2004.
101. *Fifteenth Census of the United States, 1930 Population Schedule, Fulton County, GA,* reviewed online at Ancestry.com, 2004.
102. DeVane, n.p.
103. Anonymous, "Background History," n.p.
104. Ibid.

Historical Society vacated Allenbrook in 1997, and the building remains vacant today.

Conclusion

In summary, the available evidence, though largely circumstantial, indicates that James R. King was probably the original builder and earliest tenant at Allenbrook. The date of construction was likely between 1851 and 1856; he doubtless built it to be near his new mill, the Ivy Mill. Corroborating documentation has not been uncovered to support the suggestion that John Brown, loom boss at the Ivy Mill, occupied Allenbrook during the Civil War. However, it is possible that this is true. Theophile Rochè probably never inhabited Allenbrook. After the Civil War, James R. King did not return to Allenbrook, and it is unknown who occupied it between the end of the Civil War and 1880. Nathaniel Sherman and his family were tenants at Allenbrook in 1887, and may have even lived there as early as 1880. By 1900, however, his brother, John Sherman, probably lived at Allenbrook with his wife and five daughters. Both Nathaniel and John Sherman worked at the Laurel Mill, formerly known as the Ivy Mill. John Sherman later became a shareholder in the Oxbo Road Pants Factory in Roswell. John Sherman left Allenbrook by 1903, when two families, the Copelands and the Beavers, occupied it simultaneously. At least one of these families was associated with the Laurel Mills. The Laurel Mills closed in 1911. The Laurel Mills Manufacturing Company principals sold the machinery in 1917 and the land and buildings in 1923. In 1932, an employee of Georgia Power Company, Barnett Allen Bell, purchased the part of the property on which Allenbrook stands. He and his wife renovated the building for their home and gave Allenbrook its name. In 1978, Mrs. Barnett Allen Bell sold her property to the National Park Service. The Park Service maintains the property as the gateway to the Vickery Creek Unit of the Chattahoochee River National Recreation Area.

Chronology of Development and Use

There is little doubt that Allenbrook was built as a residence and was always used as a residence until 1979. There is no real evidence that it was ever used as an office for a mill superintendent, as earlier historians suggest, although it is certainly possible that James R. King set aside one room in the house as his personal office. In 1978, Mrs. Barnett Allen Bell sold the property to the National Park Service to be a part of the new Chattahoochee River National Recreational Area. The intention was that the building was to be the entrance to the Vickery Creek unit of the Park. In 1983, an agreement was reached between the National Park Service, the Roswell Historical Society, and the City of Roswell that allowed the Historical Society to operate and maintain the house as their headquarters and as a welcome center for the city. While used by the Roswell Historical Society, the building housed a museum, a meeting room, a kitchen, a gift shop, and offices. By 1998, the Roswell Historical Society had vacated Allenbrook, and the National Park Service began stabilization, restoration, and renovation work on the building.

Original Construction

The specific construction date for Allenbrook is unknown. The building is unquestionably of antebellum construction. The exterior and bearing walls of the building are of hand-molded brick on a granite foundation. The granite foundation relates the building to other mill structures in the area. The first two factories and the contemporaneous machine shop upstream from Allenbrook were also built of brick with granite foundations. Henry Merrell mentioned that "twenty or thirty" slaves built the 1839 cotton mill,[105] so it is probable that slaves also constructed other structures. Tradition states that slaves owned by the Kings made the bricks for Allenbrook.[106] Therefore, the hand-molded bricks place the construction of the building between 1839, when the King family arrived in the area and began to build, and 1865. However, historic evidence indicates that Allenbrook was built sometime between 1851 and 1856.

Earlier historians make architectural connections between Allenbrook and other structures built by the Roswell Manufacturing Company. Walsh and Skinner, for instance, both identify the style of the house as a "saltbox" and point to the New England origins of Roswell King as the inspiration behind the design.[107] However, the building is not a saltbox style but a Plantation Plain style, which is more prevalent in Virginia and parts south, although the placement of interior chimneys rather than having chimneys on the exterior, gable ends is more typical of a New England design than a Piedmont one. Allenbrook is also unusual in that the builder articulated the Plantation Plain style in brick rather than in frame and clapboard. Walsh also cites the brick corbelling at the cornices of the building as evidence that the construction of Allenbrook occurred at approximately the same time and by the same person as other buildings associated with the Roswell Manufacturing Company.[108] The mill operatives' apartments, known as "The Bricks," built c. 1840, and the machine shop for the second cotton mill, built in 1852, do indeed have decorative brickwork at the cornices of the buildings. However, the corbelling at Allenbrook is a V-shape,

---

105. Skinner, p. 153.
106. D'Avino, n.p.
107. Walsh, passim, Skinner, p. 463, and Maynita Gerry, "Confederate House is a Pleasant Home," *Atlanta Journal Constitution*, p. 20, date unknown. Based on references in the article, it appears the article was written about 1953.
108. Walsh, p. 53.

a much more detailed decorative feature than the semi- dentil brickwork at the cornice of "The Bricks" and the machine shop. These features are sufficiently different to invalidate drawing the conclusion from the comparison that the buildings are related.

Today, the building's exterior is suggestive of its original appearance. Constructed in the Plantation Plain style – an I- house with a rear shed extension –

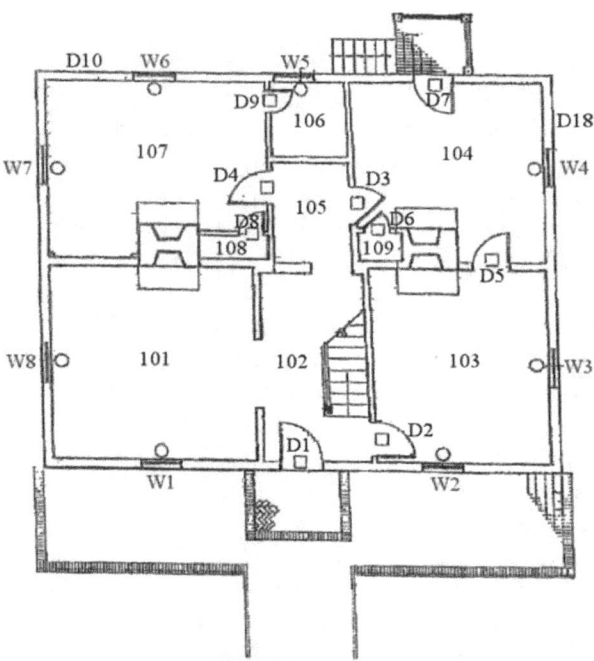

FIGURE 1. Existing First Floor Plan

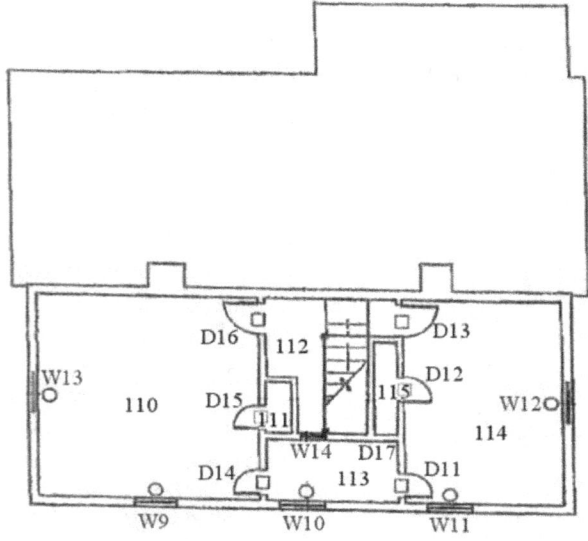

FIGURE 2. Existing Second Floor Plan

and with elements of the Greek Revival style, Allenbrook experienced few changes to its historic appearance. While some changes have been made to the exterior over the past seventy years, most, though not all, were sensitive to the building's character. The interior of the building has undergone more significant changes. However, the original plan is still evident throughout much of the house. Furthermore, a significant amount of the historic materials have been retained throughout the years. Fortunately, thanks to prudent record keeping over the past twenty- five years and to research, many of the changes made to the house can be documented and placed within a specific timeframe.

Allenbrook was constructed as a two- story building, two rooms deep on the lower story and one room deep on the upper story. The floor plan was originally rectangular, with a central hall (Room 102) dividing the first floor into east and west sections. There were four rooms on the first floor, and one, open room on the second floor. A steep and narrow set of steps with no handrails, almost a ladder, provided access to the upper floor from the central hall. There are four fireplaces in the building, one located in each of the four rooms on the first floor. There are two chimneys providing flues for the fireplaces, symmetrically located on the north side of the two- story portion of the building, which faces south. The interior flooring is wide, heart-pine boards.

The building is constructed of hand- made brick on a continuous granite foundation. An interesting feature of the brick walls is the presence of painted white penciling marks in the mortar joints. Penciling was a common nineteenth- century decorative treatment, where the mortar joints of bricks were painted to give the appearance of thin, more precise joints. There is evidence of these white lines on the west, south, and east elevations. The building has a hipped roof over the main, two- story portion, and a shed roof over the rear extension. The exterior brick walls indicate that the extension is an original feature of the building, not an addition. Saw marks on the historic wood roof framing and some interior wall framing indicates the use of both sash and circular saws. The Roswell Manufacturing Company holdings by 1851 included both a brick kiln and a sawmill that likely provided raw materials for the building. Historically, Allenbrook had a one-story porch supported by brick piers and covered with a hipped roof that sheltered the front door and both windows on the first story. A shadow line of this porch is evident over the front entrance to the house. A watercolor painted by Barnett A. Bell in 1932 documents the existence of the porch.[109] This is the only known pictorial evidence of the porch. Although consistent with the original nineteenth-century Plantation Plain style of Allenbrook, it is unknown whether this porch was constructed with the house or was a later addition.

Examination of the existing features of the house, in consideration of its presumed original floor plan, reveals that there were likely thirteen double hung windows in the house when first constructed. Most of the existing window openings appear original to the house and include window openings 1 through 4 and 6 through 13. According to the Barnett Bell's 1932 watercolor, a window was originally located on the north elevation of the house where Door 7 currently exists. The original window openings are larger in size than those added later. The locations of the original doors of the house are more difficult to confirm, as changes made to the floor plan involved both the addition of new rooms and the modification of existing door openings. However, it appears that door openings 1, 2, 3, and 4 were all original, given the presumed earliest floor plan of the house. Additionally, door opening 5 may be an original opening, as the door hanging in the opening is a two-panel door similar to Doors 2, 3 and 4. The two-panel doors all have two vertical, flat panels, a configuration commonly seen in eighteenth-century domestic architecture. Two other doors are known to have originally existed in the house. A door was located on the north elevation of the house where Window 5 currently exists. Evidence of this includes Barnett Bell's 1932 watercolor, and photographs included in Ali Miri's 1994 report showing brick patching in the north wall beneath Window 5. Also, a small door opening was located in the east wall of the first floor hall, beneath the stairs, and led to the dining room, Room 103. Furthermore, the arched opening to Room 101, while known to be a later modification, includes the original opening to the room.

There is evidence of white paint on most of the historic shingle lath and the rafters exposed on the interior of the shed rooms. While some of the shingle lath is unpainted, yet appear aged, the absence of unused nail holes in the painted lath indicates that they were not recycled from another structure for use in Allenbrook. Therefore, it appears that the shed rooms did not originally have a finished ceiling, and the exposed roof structure was painted.

Later Alterations

The shed section at the north of the house has been subjected to significant changes over the years. Many of the earlier finishes have been removed, complicating interpretation of the chronological development of the house. The fact that there are two fireplaces in this portion of the house indicates that the shed area has likely always been partitioned in some fashion and was probably never a single room. The north walls of Rooms 106 and 107 were completely rebuilt by the National Park Service between 1998 and 2002, and are currently unfinished, so these do not provide information regarding earlier construction and finishes. The remaining wall finishes in the rear shed rooms aid in understanding how this section of the house evolved. Where intact, the original walls of Room 104 are finished plaster on lath painted white up to the exposed shed roof structure, indicating the

FIGURE 3. Living Room (Room 101), published in Atlanta Constitution, 1957. Source: Roswell Historical Society.

109. The 1932 watercolor of Allenbrook is signed "Barnett A. Bell" and is included in the Bell Family scrapbook for the renovation of the house. The scrapbook is held by the Roswell Historical Society Archives, Roswell, Georgia.

there was no lowered ceiling in this room. Likewise, the original west and south walls in Room 107 and the south wall of what is now known as Room 108 are finished with plaster and white paint up to the shed roof structure, indicating that this room also originally did not have a lowered ceiling. The south wall of Room 105, above the door opening, is finished with an unpainted, mottled, reddish-brown skim coat, apparently of plaster. This variation from the south walls to the east and west indicates that, at some point, walls extended to the roofline on either side of this section, forming a rear hall like the front hall. This rear hall existed when the Bell family purchased Allenbrook, and is believed to have been original to the house. Because the presence of painted shingle lath over the entire shed area indicates that it was originally exposed to the interior, including in the rear hall, it is reasonable to assume that the walls of the rear hall may have once been finished up to the roofline. The upper portion of the east wall of the rear hall, above the former ceiling level, is currently unfinished revealing the wood lath and plaster keys of the west wall of Room 104 and the exposed framing of the east wall of the rear hall. If they existed, finishes of the upper portions of the walls in the rear hall, Rooms 105 and 106, deteriorated and/or were removed at some unidentified time. The variation of the wall finishes above the level of the ceilings installed by the Bell family indicates that a lowered ceiling was installed in the hall at some point after the original construction of the house, though it is unclear when this installation occurred. The lowered ceiling may have been installed during the occupancy of the James R. King family in the 1850s and early 1860s, or it might have been installed after 1932. Since it is currently missing, it is not possible to accurately date the installation of the lowered ceiling in the hall, although it is possible to definitively state that there was one.

Barnett Bell Renovation

Barnett Allen Bell "restored" Allenbrook sometime in the 1930s, after purchasing the house in 1932. The work undertaken by the Bells is more correctly called a renovation, especially since it involved more new construction than restoration of historic features. Part of the renovation included the addition of a bathroom (Room 106) at the north end of the hall on the first floor, between the two shed rooms (Rooms 104 and 107). This involved the addition of a wall dividing the rear hall into two rooms. At this time the rear door to the central hall was removed and a window (Window 5) was created in its place. The north window in Room 104 was removed, and a door was created (Door 7). A closet was added in each of Rooms 104 and 107. The door opening in the east wall of the first floor hall, beneath the second floor landing, and which led to Room 103, was closed and a built-in case with shelves was constructed in its place in Room 103. The renovations made to the first floor added four new doors and one new window to the building, while two existing doors and one existing window were removed. Doors 6 through 9 and Window 5 were all added at this time.

Additional changes were made to the first floor of the house during this period. According to Barnett Bell's handwritten note, they installed the arched doorway in the living room, Room 101, and constructed the existing stairs, including the handrail leading to the top of the steps and along the upper landing. This staircase replaced a set of steeply-pitched steps only 18" wide and without a railing that led to the upper floor. These steps faced in the opposite direction from the current stairs. Further, Mr. Bell notes the origin and date of the newel post located at the base of the staircase. It was relocated from the Glades Plantation, home of Major John Bell, and dates to 1840.

According to the 1957 Atlanta Constitution article on Allenbrook, the Bells replaced the hearths at the fireplaces using fieldstone to complement the existing heart-pine floors.[110] Additionally, Barnett

FIGURE 4. Kitchen (Room 104), 1984. Source: Roswell Historical Society.

Bell's handwritten note identifies the mantel in the living room (Room 101) as dating to the post- 1930 work and the pine mantel in the sitting room (Room 107) as original to the house. The mantel in the dining room (Room 103) is very similar to that in Room 101 and, although not stated in the article or in the note, may have also been installed by the Bell family. Likewise, the pine mantel in the kitchen is identical to that in the sitting room and, therefore, is likely original to the house. All of the mantels were painted except for the one in the sitting room. The Bells removed the layers of paint from this mantel down to the original heart- pine wood and polished it with linseed oil and wax.

Crown and base molding were installed throughout the interior during the 1930s. The first finished ceilings may have been installed in the shed rooms at this time, as well. It is clear from both photographic and physical evidence that finished ceilings existed throughout the shed rooms by the 1950s. Photographs taken of the interior in 1957 and 1984 illustrate the former ceiling and crown molding conditions of Rooms 104 and 107. The varied paint scheme, the finishes, and the exposed framing currently existing in these rooms reveals significant information about their evolution. A ceiling of plaster on lath was first installed, following the pitch of the roof, in Room 104 and its closet, 109. This is evidenced by the presence of severely deteriorated lath nailed to the roof rafters and partly covered by remnants of plaster in Room 109 and by crown molding remaining along the interior roofline in Room 104. Another ceiling of plasterboard was, apparently, later applied directly to the roof rafters after removal of the old ceiling of lath and plaster. This is supported by the presence of paper remnants nailed to the roof framing in this room, indicating that, at some time, the ceiling was likely plasterboard. This ceiling was not installed in Room 109; therefore, it was installed in Room 104, after Room 109 was built. It is possible that the plaster- on- lath ceiling once present in these rooms also predated the existence of the closet, Room 109.

The finished ceilings installed in Rooms 106, 107 and 108 were horizontally installed and lower. Evidence of this includes the shadow lines where crown molding once existed, found two- thirds of the way up the west and south walls of Room 107. A further

indication of this former ceiling is the truncated walls in these rooms. The east, west, and north walls of Room 105, the south and west walls of Room 106, the east wall of Room 107, and the north and east walls of Room 108 rise only to the approximate level of the crown molding shadow lines in Room 107. The presence of this lowered ceiling provided for attic space above, probably accessed via Room 108, the closet in Room 107. The truncated walls in Rooms 105, 106, 107 and 108 reveal similar framing conditions, indicating they were likely installed contemporaneously. A horizontal framing member is attached to the south walls of Room 105 and 108, just above the level of the former ceilings. The framing indicates that the Bells likely rebuilt the east wall of Room 107 as part of their remodeling efforts. This is supported by the fact that framing for the east wall of Rooms 106 and 107 above the ceiling level no longer exists. Since the differential wall finishes of the south walls of Rooms 105, 107, and 108 indicate that the east wall of Room 107 once extended to the roofline, it appears that the Bells rebuilt rather than remodeled the wall, making it shorter in the process. The wall between Rooms 105 and 106 was then built to the same height as this shorter wall, and the lowered ceilings installed over at least Rooms 106, 107, and 108, and possibly over 105.

A shadow on the floorboards in the first floor hall indicates that a door may have once separated the front (Room 102) and rear halls (Room 105/106). After the door, trim and framing were removed, the walls and the remainder of the opening were

FIGURE 5. Sitting Room (Room 107), published in Atlanta Constitution, 1957. Source: Roswell Historical Society.

110. Richards, 1957.

refinished. A variation in the baseboard on the north wall of Room 102 provides supporting evidence for the possible existence of an earlier door at this location. As stated earlier, the Bells installed all of the base and crown molding in the house sometime after 1932. The east end of the baseboard on the north wall of Room 102 is actually plaster, molded to resemble the adjacent baseboard. While no similar evidence exists in the baseboards of the opposite wall, the presence of this feature along with the shadow on the floorboards, supports the possibility of an earlier door. This door is not mentioned in the existing documentation of changes made by the Bell family. It is likely that it either predated the Bells or was installed by them during their renovation efforts, given that the repair made to the baseboard clearly occurred sometime after 1932.

Although all of the interior door and window trim, base and crown molding, treads and risers of the interior stairs, and the two fireplace mantels added by the Bells in Rooms 101 and 103 are currently painted a medium blue, historic photographs of the interior included in the Atlanta Constitution article from 1957 reveal that the crown molding and mantels that were painted were a lighter color, possibly white. Additionally, these photographs indicate that the chimney breasts on both the Room 101 and Room 107 fireplaces were painted a light color, possibly white, and the associated fireboxes were painted a dark color, likely black. The walls illustrated in the photographs appear to be white.

According to the anonymous researcher who interviewed Barnett Bell, Jr. in 1980, the upper floor when the Bells purchased the house was open space accessed by a steep and narrow set of stairs without handrails. In his handwritten note, Barnett Bell refers to the upper floor as a "loft." While it may seem unusual that families with several children lived in this building without installing some partitioning in this area, there is no physical evidence to support that this occurred, and there is written evidence to support that it did not.

An interesting feature of the upper hall is the significant step-up located on either side of the landing at the top of the stairs. This feature may have been necessitated by the change in orientation of the stairs. According to Barnett Bell, the stairs to the second floor originally began near the middle of the house and ascended toward the south, or front.

However, when the Bells installed the new stairs, they oriented them in the opposite direction. The need to reduce the pitch of the stairs while keeping the door to the east room on the first floor clear may have resulted in a stairway that reached the upstairs back wall one step short of the upper level. This made it necessary to incorporate a step on both sides of the landing to access the rooms on either side. However, it is also possible that the stairs were intentionally designed in this fashion.

The Bells entirely reconfigured the second floor during the post-1930 renovation. The open space was divided into three rooms, two closets, and a hall. Some physical characteristics support the written documentation that the upper floor was originally one large open space. The floorboards throughout the entire second floor are all similarly sized and run in the same direction, with no breaks at the room divisions. There is no evidence in the floorboards the rooms were ever partitioned other than as they are now. Additionally, examination of the deteriorated wall finish in the stairwell at the second floor level reveals that the wall may be finished plaster on gypsum or plaster board instead of the plaster on wood lath of the original walls, as no lath was observed in the exposed section of this wall. However, the deteriorated section is small, limiting visual access. The scope of work for this report calls for non-destructive inspection, so it was not possible to remove additional portions of the wall to inspect the underlying construction. Used as early as 1900, plaster on gypsum board lath is commonly seen in houses built in the 1920s and 30s and by the mid-1940s predominates over the use of plaster on wood lath. While this finding supports the presumed date of the second floor walls, wood lath and plaster keys can be observed in several of the upper floor walls that are presumed added by the Bells. These walls include the east wall of Room 110 and the west wall of Room 114. This condition can be observed through the attic access in the closet, Room 111, and the attic access in the bathroom, Room 113. The Bell family renovated the first floor shed rooms with plaster on lath walls. Therefore, it is probable that they renovated the second floor "loft area" using the similar construction materials. If the exposed portion of the wall is, in fact, constructed of plasterboard, and not plaster on lath, it is probable that the upper portion of the east wall of the stairwell was refinished at some point after the initial renovations undertaken by the Bells. Additional physical evidence of the subdivision of second floor includes the base and crown molding and all of the room and closet doors. The molding and doors match those installed in the first floor rooms after 1930. This evidence supports the written documentation that this area of the house was originally an open loft and was modified by the Bells.

The reconfiguration of the second floor introduced seven new doors (Doors 11 through 17) and one new window (Window 14) to the building. The doors leading to the renovated spaces in the house are similar in design with the exception of Door 17, which is a small, board- and- batten door leading to the second story attic. Doors 8, 9, 11, 12, 13, 14, 15 and 16 all have five, equally- spaced panels running horizontally from the top to the bottom, and machine- molded stiles and rails. These characteristics are indicative of early twentieth century door styles and, therefore, support that the Bell family installed them when they renovated the interior of the house.

Plumbing and electricity were installed in the house during the post- 1930 renovation. Throughout the house are features of this original service, including the bathtub, toilet, and sink in the upstairs bathroom and lighting fixtures and/or fittings in Rooms 101, 110, and 113. Wall sconces were installed on either side of the arched opening in the east wall of Room 101, and a cast iron sconce was installed to the right of Door 16 on the east wall of Room 110. A small, ceramic fixture was installed above the sink in Room 113 at this time as well. An interesting feature of the stairway is the electric light fixture installed on top of the newel post at the top of the stairway. It is probable that the Bell family installed this fixture when the other electrical lights were installed.

Additional modifications were made to the exterior of the house in the 1930s and 1940s. It appears that the existing board- and- batten shutters were installed at this time. While evident in the 1940 photographs of Allenbrook, window shutters are not depicted in the 1932 watercolor painted by Barnett Bell. A photograph dating to 1957 shows board- and- batten shutters, matching those on the windows, flanking the front door. The shutters are not evident in the 1940 photograph of the house, indicating the door shutters were installed between 1940 and 1957. A photograph printed in an unnamed

newspaper believed to date to sometime in 1983, based on extrapolated information, shows these shutters.[III] A 1984 photograph of the house reveals that the shutters had been removed sometime in 1983 or 1984.

These two watercolors were likely painted by Bell from memory some time after the renovations. The strongest evidence of this is the depiction of the windows. Amateur artists drawing houses from

FIGURE 6. Watercolor of Allenbrook by Barnett A. Bell, Front Elevation. Courtesy of Roswell Historical Society Archives.

FIGURE 7. Watercolor of Allenbrook by Barnett A. Bell, Courtesy of Roswell Historical Society Archives.

111. Mohr, Merri Ann. "Allenbrook Restoration Awaits Funding." unknown newspaper, circa 1983., page 68. Copy found in Roswell Historical Society Archives.

memory often depict six over six windows as three over three. They recall that the window frame has six panes; they often forget that a double- hung window has two frames. Bell also had difficulty depicting the hipped roof of the porch properly, most likely because he was not viewing it at the time he painted it. Because this painting was probably

FIGURE 10. South elevation, 1940. Source: Roswell Historical Society.

FIGURE 11. North elevation and rear yard, 1940. Source: Roswell Historical Society.

not painted until after the changes were made, using these watercolors to recreate the exterior appearance of the building should be with extreme caution.

According to documentation included in the Allenbrook papers on file at the National Park Service, the one- story porch with the hipped roof was removed shortly after the Bell family moved into the house.[112] A small porch with a gabled roof was constructed in its place. Supporting the roof are two square posts at its outer edge. Flanking the doorway are two square pilasters. The shadow line of the porch roof and pilasters are still evident around the front door. This second porch was not long lived, however, as a photograph of the house dated circa 1950s illustrates a full- length, full- height porch on the front elevation. This porch had a flat roof without a finished ceiling and was supported by square columns and a brick floor. A shadow line of this feature is visible beneath the cornice on the south elevation of the house. The brick stoop constructed by the Bells on the north elevation at the newly created rear entrance is shown in a 1940 photograph. The railing appears to have originally consisted of no more than metal pipes spanning the bracketed roof supports and extending to the exterior north wall and down the north side of the granite steps. Today, the National Park Service has constructed a new wood railing with square balusters on the rear stoop, but there are other existing details that differ from the apparent original conditions. The existing bracketed square columns are fluted and are larger than the wood posts in the 1940 photograph. Also, the rear door is currently surrounded with wood trim, and a fluted wood pilaster is located to the east of the door. Neither of these features is present in the 1940 photograph. Based on Ali Miri's 1994 report, these features were, however, present in 1994, along with a wood railing with square balusters, matching that, which exists today. It is reasonable to suggest that, when the second, gabled front porch was dismantled to build the third two- story porch, the square columns and one of the pilasters were reused on the rear porch. Additionally, it is likely that the pipe railing was changed to the existing style at that time.

Existing documentation reveals that the site of Allenbrook when the Bell family occupied the

112. Anonymous, "Background History." n.p.

house varied from that which exists today. The Bells made significant changes to the site. This included raising the ground level and paving the porch area in front of the house "with brick salvaged from the old mill,"[113] as well as creating a "terrace" in the back. This site work is illustrated in the 1940 photographs. The terrace appears to be of stone, possibly the same granite that was used in the construction of foundations for the Ivy/Laurel Mill structures. They spent five years clearing the underbrush from the back of their house to the edge of the creek. Today, the historic bricks and pavers have been removed in both the front and rear yard. In 1978, Mrs. Barnett Bell had the Allenbrook property surveyed. This survey shows a drive that encircles the house and extends southwest to Atlanta Road. It is unknown if this drive was an historic feature of the property that predated the Bell family. However, it appears in the 1940 photograph, unpaved but edged with bricks set at a 45- degree angle. The entrance to this drive from Atlanta Road still exists.

NPS Treatment

In 1978, the National Park Service acquired Allenbrook and the surrounding land for inclusion in the Chattahoochee National Recreation Area. In 1983, the Roswell Historical Society reached an agreement with the National Park Service to lease Allenbrook for its offices and as the Roswell Welcome Center. During their tenancy, the Roswell Historical Society renovated the building, installing a new gypsum board ceiling in the upstairs, eastern bedroom, Room 114, and in the dining room, Room 103. In addition, new telephone lines, power outlets, and lighting were installed to support their office functions. The board- and batten shutters flanking the front door were removed. At some point during their occupation, the Roswell Historical Society painted a floor cloth on the floor of the downstairs hall. Text included in one of the Society's past brochures on Allenbrook states that the floor cloth was stenciled as an interpretation of decorative treatments typical of homes of similar vintage. There is no physical evidence that this interpretive treatment is historically accurate for Allenbrook. In addition to renovations, continued maintenance of the building during this period was achieved

through the cooperation of the Roswell Historical Society and the National Park Service. According to their records, some of the maintenance included repairing some of the windows, installing commercial- grade carpet throughout and vinyl flooring in the kitchen, replacing the baseboard on the south wall of the dining room, Room 103 due to water damage, painting, and managing insect infestation.

Ali Miri's 1994 report inventoried the building materials and documented the most significant problems with the building. The problems identified were 1) a lack of drainage around the building, 2) cracks in the north wall of the building caused by expansion and contraction of the clay floor beneath, 3) the unfinished concrete block basement wall, 4) temporary wood and metal support posts in basement, 5) bulging on the lower part of the north wall at the basement door and 6) various site and driveway improvements needed. Between 1998 and 2002 the National Park Service undertook a series of stabilization and rehabilitation treatments to the house, many of which addressed the problems identified in Ali Miri's report. The treatments were primarily completed over the course of two rehabilitation campaigns, 1998 to 1999 and 2000 to 2002, and included:

- Reconstructing the north wall of the house.

- Repointing masonry joints where needed due to prior inappropriate repair treatments. All new mortar matches the original in color,

FIGURE 14. Southeast elevation, circa 1940s. Source: Roswell Historical Society.

---

113. Richards, 1957.

material, and application as identified in an analysis completed in 2001; however, some of the historic mortar on the north elevation was different in color from the original. The contractor did not replicate this historic brick and mortar patching beneath Window 5 or the historic penciling.

■ Installing a continuous concrete footing beneath the north wall foundation.

■ Supplementing the roof structure and reconstructing the floor structure in the rear extension.

■ Constructing full- height, cement- block walls in the basement.

■ Installing an interior support beam and columns in the basement.

■ Installing a vapor barrier in the crawl space beneath the south end of the house and metal vents in the north wall of the basement.

■ Installing new doors to the basement.

■ Restoring the window sashes.

■ Reglazing the windows.

■ Replacing the exterior doors and door frames.

■ Replacing the sill at the front door.

■ Replacing two window frames (Windows 5 and 6).

■ Installing new hardware on all the windows, shutters, and exterior doors.

■ Installing wood framed, screened doors on the two main exterior doors.

■ Installing interior storm windows on all the exterior windows.

■ Removing the ceilings throughout the shed rooms (Rooms 104, 105, 106, 107, 108 and 109).

■ Removing and storing the crown moldings throughout the shed rooms (Rooms 104, 105, 106, 107, 108 and 109).

■ Removing all appliances and plumbing fixtures from the first floor.

■ Removing the furnace.

■ Replacing damaged wooden roof shingles with like materials.

■ Installing gutters and downspouts on the north and south elevations of the house, and installing drainage pipes beneath the north end of the house.

■ Regrading the east, south, and west sides of the house to divert water away from the building.

■ Removing the historic brick pavers in the south and north yard and installing a brick pad outside the front door (south elevation), and a path leading to the existing Park parking lot.

■ Removing vegetative growth from east elevation and northeast corner of house.

■ Painting the exterior windows, shutters, and doors.

■ Installing foil radiant barriers and cellulose insulation in the attic.

■ Reconstructing portions of the roof framing,.

■ Repairing the chimney bases.

■ Installing interior storm windows in all the window openings.

■ Installing new HVAC equipment and a security system.

The building currently remains vacant yet maintained by the National Park Service. The past treatments undertaken by the Park successfully stabilized the building. However, some of the work completed resulted in a loss of some of the historic finishes such as the characteristic brick patching on the north exterior wall, as well as the ceilings and some of the interior wall finishes in the shed rooms. Additionally, changes were made to the site, including the abandonment of the historic drive and the removal of the historic pavers in both the front and rear yard. Although, the removal of these finishes was largely necessitated by the stabilization and current use priorities, it will be important to reintroduce some of the historic features for interpretation.

Physical Description

The following section is a physical description of Allenbrook as it currently exists (2004). Significant changes made to the building and their estimated age are identified where applicable. For a more detailed history of these changes, please consult the "Chronology of Development and Use" section of this report.

Summary of Historic Character

Located on a bluff on the north side of State Route 9 (Atlanta Street), Allenbrook is situated on a wooded lot southwest of Big (Vickery) Creek. The house faces south. A vegetative buffer exists between the house and Atlanta Street and to the west of the house. To the rear (north) of the house is a gently sloping lawn, which abuts a walking trail, part of the National Park Service's Vickery Creek unit of the Chattahoochee River National Recreation Area. To the east of the house is a grassed area bordered by sporadic vegetation. A brick pathway leads from the National Park Service parking area located to the east of Allenbrook and extends to the brick patio at the front of the house. The mill ruins with which Allenbrook is associated are located to the southeast of the house, east of the intersections of Atlanta Street (which becomes Roswell Road), Riverside Road, and Azalea Drive.

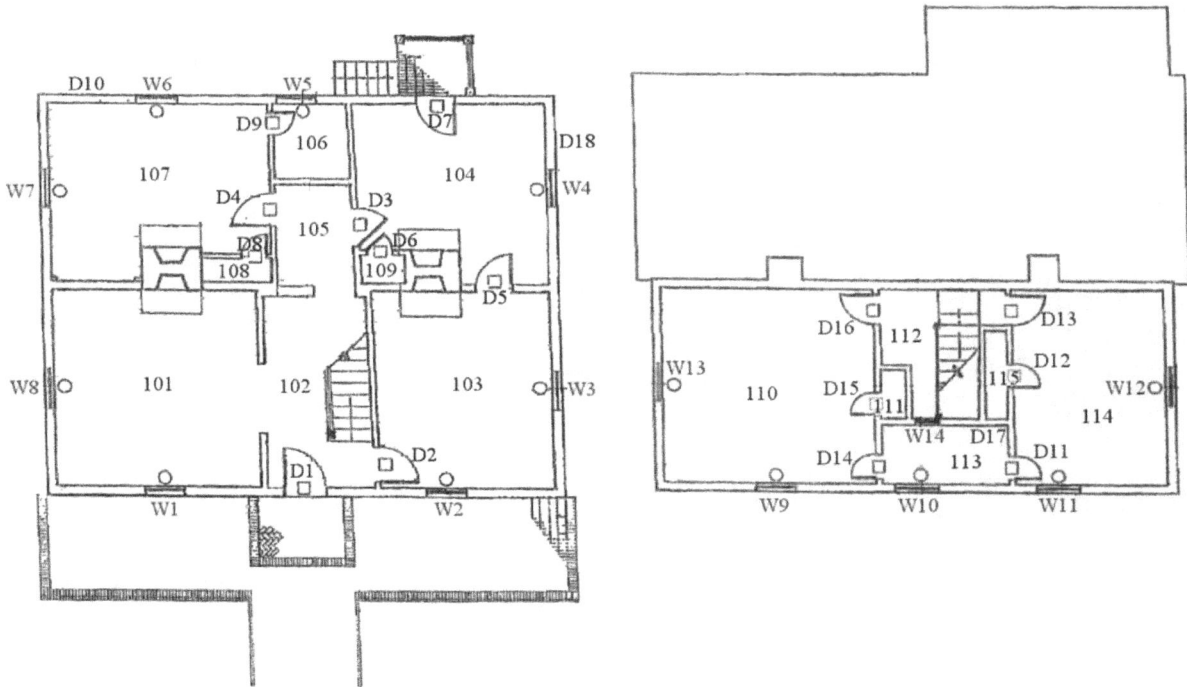

FIGURE 16. Existing first floor plan, left, and second floor plan, right.

FIGURE 17. Concrete block retaining wall along south side of excavated basement.

FIGURE 18. New 2" by 10" supplementary support beams at north, two-story wall.

FIGURE 19. Bricks stacked in basement.

Allenbrook is a two-story, brick I-house with a rear shed. This configuration is regionally known as the Plantation Plain style. The building has a rectangular floor plan, both hipped and shed roofs, two central chimneys, and a granite foundation. The house has eleven rooms and four closets. Located above the second story is an attic space running the full length and width of the second floor. There are eighteen doors, fourteen windows, and four brick fireplaces in the house. On the rear elevation of the house is a stoop covered by a shed roof supported by square columns.

The interior of the house is divided into seven rooms on the first floor and four rooms on the second floor. From the front of the house to the back, the first floor consists of two rooms (Rooms 101 and 103) flanking a central hall (Room 102) followed by another pair of rooms (Rooms 104 and 107) flanking a central hall (Room 105) and a bathroom (Room 106). A staircase is located along the east wall of the front hall (Room 102) and leads to the second floor hall (Room 112). To the south of the hall is the upstairs bathroom (Room 113). Flanking the upstairs hall and bathroom are two bedrooms (Rooms 110 and 114). The house has four closets, two on the first floor (Rooms 108 and 109) and two on the second floor (Rooms 111 and 115). See illustrations on the following page.

Structural System

There is limited accessibility to the structural framing of Allenbrook. Portions of the floor, roof, and wall structures were exposed, and therefore, were assessed. Much of the first floor framing has been reconstructed. Likewise, the hipped roof framing that was visible was largely reconstructed. The historic shed roof framing is intact, but has been supplemented with new members. As most of the wall framing is concealed by the wall finishes, it is presumed that the historic fabric is largely intact. Portions of the wall framing in the shed rooms and stairwell have been reconstructed.

All measurements of new framing members provided in this section are nominal, unless otherwise noted. Measurements of historic framing are actual unless otherwise noted.

Foundation

Originally a continuous rubble stone (granite) wall bearing on clay, the foundation of Allenbrook has been largely reconstructed using both historic and new materials along the entire north elevation and along portions of the east and west elevations. During the National Park Service stabilization work completed between 2000 and 2002, a continuous 28" by 14" concrete footing was constructed beneath these walls, with three #5 rebar running horizontal 2" from the bottom of the footing. Bearing on these footers are foundation walls constructed of 7½" by 1'- 3½" concrete blocks (CMU).

Prior to the 2000- 2002 stabilization, the granite foundation walls were partially braced along the interior by a concrete block wall. The concrete wall installed between 2000 and 2002 extends along the inside of the granite foundation wall along the entire north side and along portions of the east and west sides of the shed area of the house. The east and west walls connect with a concrete retaining wall that has been constructed along the south side of the basement area. A section of this wall projects further to the south than the rest of the retaining wall, possibly to accommodate the HVAC equipment.

Between 2000 and 2002, a series of columns and a beam were installed south of the inside face of the reconstructed north wall. According to National Park Service drawings, each column is supported by a concrete footing measuring 24" by 24" by 12". In addition, drawings indicate that the National Park Service installed two 2" by 10" supplementary support beams abutting the historic, load- bearing granite foundation wall beneath the north, two-story wall. This rubble wall provides foundation support for the fireplaces and walls above. The 2" by 10" support beams are supported by concrete blocks and shims on undisturbed soil.

Access to the building foundation and basement is through Door 10 and down a small set of frame steps constructed by the National Park Service. Of particular note is a stack of bricks located adjacent to the stairs in the basement. It is presumed that these bricks are some of those salvaged from the site work on the front and rear yards during the stabilization and rehabilitation treatments undertaken by the National Park Service between 1998 and 2002.

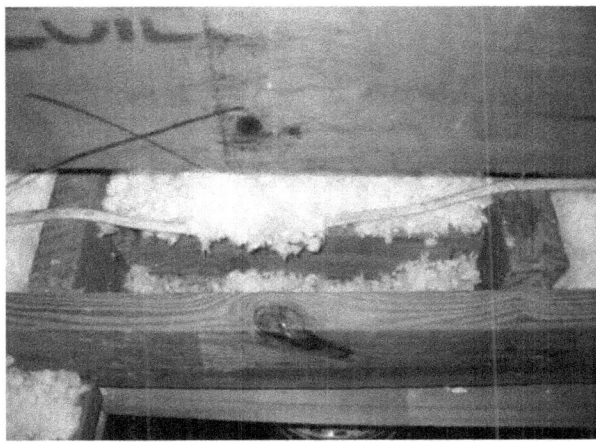

FIGURE 20. Floor joists in attic.

FIGURE 21. New north wall framing in Room 104.

FIGURE 22. East wall of stairwell in Room 102. Note gypsum board wall finish.

Floor Framing

The first floor framing is only visible in the excavated basement under the north third of the building. Visible in the basement are new 2" by 10" joists spaced at approximately 15" to 16" on center. The joists span from the top of the new, concrete block, north wall to the historic rubble, load-bearing wall and adjacent supplementary 2" by 10"

FIGURE 23. Posts and beam providing central support to hipped roof.

FIGURE 24. Shed roof framing as seen from Room 106.

support beams beneath the north two-story wall. A new 2" by 6" sill plate is bolted to the top of the concrete block walls along the north, east, and west elevations. A new 2" by 4" sill plate is joined to the 2" by 10" supplementary support beams at the rubble, load-bearing wall. Rolled batt insulation has been installed between the joists. This floor framing and insulation dates to the 2000-2002 National Park Service stabilization work. Beyond the concrete block retaining wall installed between 2000 and 2002, a very shallow crawl space exists. The limited height of this space and the presence of the concrete block wall prevented access to the southern half of the first floor framing. The only historic materials observed from this vantage were the granite rubble stone foundations of the chimneys and the north wall of the two-story portion of the building. All of the floor framing observed in this area appeared new but could not be reached for measurement.

Finished ceilings in the first floor rooms conceal the second floor framing. However, the depth of the second floor header at the stairs is 9¼". Given the 1" thickness of the floorboards above, the joists must measure approximately 8" deep. Ali Miri's 1994 report indicates that the joists are 2" by 8".

Examination of the nails in the floorboards above reveals the joists are likely spaced approximately 24" on center.

Wall Framing

At the perimeter of the house and at the two-story interior masonry wall, the walls are load-bearing masonry. The structural integrity of the solid masonry exterior walls is enhanced by a header course every three courses of running bond. The interior wall structure is only revealed in a few places throughout the house. A portion of the east wall in Room 102, along the stairway, has been removed to reveal the wall structure and interior plumbing. The studs at this location are circular sawn, measure 2" by 4", nominal, and are spaced approximately 16" on center. The Bell family opened this wall during renovations to accommodate plumbing. The finish material at this location is gypsum board that was installed as a patch to the wall. Also, where the truncated walls exist in Room 105, the top plate is exposed. These historic members measure 2" by 4", and date to the renovation work done by the Bell family. The framing of the north wall in Room 104 is exposed and measures 2" by 4", nominal, spaced 16" on center. This wall was entirely rebuilt by the National Park Service contractor between 2000 and 2004.

Roof Framing

Due to the recent stabilization treatments made by the National Park Service in the attic, including a foil radiant barrier applied to the underside of the roof and duct work and blown cellulose fiber insulation installed throughout, very limited access is available to the framing of the main hipped roof. Most of the framing that is visible may be seen through the access in the ceiling of Room 114. The framing that is visible is almost entirely new, including 2" by 4" posts spaced at 15" on center, serving as vertical ridge support. These posts bear on two beams sistered together, measuring 2" by 6" and 2" by 10" and running east to west.

The shed roof framing is exposed to the interior of Rooms 104 through 109. 2" by 7" rafters, spaced at 15" on center exist which appear historic. Supplementing the historic framing are new 2" by 8" rafters sistered to some of the historic rafters. At the north wall beam, new 2" by 10" boards have been sistered to the rafters to provide additional support to the roof structure.

The shed roof framing over the north stoop is comprised of new 2" by 4" rafters spaced at 22½" on center. This roof structure was reconstructed between 2000 and 2002, by the National Park Service contractor.

Exterior Finishes

Stoop

Located on the north elevation at the rear entrance to the building (Door 7), approximately 6'- 3½" from the eastern end, is a covered stoop. At its northern end, the stoop measures 5'- 4" square by 3'- 3½" tall. The ground rises toward the front, or south side, of the house. Due to this incline, the stoop measures approximately 3'- 0" tall at its southern end. The stoop is constructed of dark red bricks measuring approximately 3" by 8", and is accessed from the west by granite stairs. This brick is darker in shade that those used on the balance of the exterior walls. The stairs are comprised of randomly- sized stones joined with mortar. The stones measure 2" to 3" thick, 10" to 14" wide and 8" to 16" in length. The

height of the stairs is 2'- 7½", and there are five stairs to the stoop. The stairs are comprised of five 6½" risers and five 11" treads. A balustrade extends up the north side of the stairs. The balusters measure 1" square and are spaced at 4" on center. The rails measure 4" by 2" by 5'- 9" long. Located at the top and bottom of the balustrade is a newel post, measuring 3½" square and 3'- 7" tall. The top 2" sections of the newel posts are a pyramidal shape. It

FIGURE 25. Framing for shed roof at rear stoop.

FIGURE 26. Stoop at rear entrance to house.

is known that the stoop was constructed sometime after 1932 by the Bell family. The stoop was dismantled when the National Park Service contractor reconstructed the north wall between 2000 and 2002. All of the materials on the stoop are historic with the exception of the balustrade, which

FIGURE 27. Detail of column base.

FIGURE 28. Stoop located at rear entrance to house.

was constructed between 2000 and 2002 by the National Park Service contractor.

A shed roof covers the stoop. A National Park Service contractor reconstructed this roof between 2000 and 2002. Supporting the shed roof at the stoop are three historic columns, one of which is engaged in the southern wall of the house. This engaged column, or pilaster, measures approximately 8" by 4" by 7'- 3¾". The remaining two columns measure 8½" square by 7'- 3¾" tall. Both the pilaster and columns have square shafts with a simple base and capital, derivative of the Tuscan order. The lower surfaces of the shafts are fluted. The flutes measure 1" by 3'- 10". Each of these columns has one bracket at the top, which frames into the beam above, providing additional support to the roof structure. The brackets measure 3½" square and 2'- 1½" long. Spanning the columns on the east, north, and a portion of the west sides of the stoop is a balustrade. The balusters measure 1" square and are largely spaced at 4" on center. The rails measure 2" by 4" and, from the east side to the west side of the stoop, measure 4'- 2½", 4'- 9" and 1'- 0¾" long. The balustrades along the stoop and the stairs are new features of the building installed between 2000 and 2002 by the National Park Service contractor.

Walls

The exterior walls of the house are load- bearing, masonry walls of hand- molded red brick laid primarily in a pattern of three courses of running bond to one course of header bond, called a four course common bond. The exterior brick dimensions are approximately 3" by 8". The brick is lighter in color than that used to construct the stoop on the north elevation. On the east, south and west elevations are penciling marks in the historic mortar joints. The penciling is white, painted lines applied to the joints to give the brick walls a more finished appearance, an historic treatment. The lower portion of the exterior walls on the north, east, and west elevations are constructed of rubble stone (granite) of random sizes. This stonework defines the basement level of the house. The height of the stonework varies with the surrounding grade. Along the north elevation, the granite wall extends approximately 3'- 8½" above grade. Along the east and west elevations, it extends from 3'- 0" above grade at the northern end of the walls to approximately 3" to 4" above grade towards the southern end of the walls. The stones measure 2" to 6" thick and 10" to 16" long.

Located along the eaves of the south, east, and west walls and along the two- story north wall is decorative brick corbelling in a v- shaped pattern. From the bottom of each v- shape, the pattern is comprised of three brick courses, beginning with one header at the bottom, followed by two headers and finishing with one header and one stretcher. Two continuous courses of brick are above the corbelling.

Flat arches form the head of the window openings on the south, east, and west elevations. A flat arch is also over Door 1 on the south elevation. On the south elevation, the arches are comprised of two soldier courses of brick and measure approximately 1'- 4" wide and 3'- 4" long. The arches vary on the east and west elevations. On the two- story walls of the east and west elevations, the arches are like those located on the south elevation. The window arches located in the shed walls of the east and west elevations are approximately 8" wide and 3'- 0" long.

On the south elevation, just below the second story windows, are shadow lines of two of the former porch roofs. The National Park Service contractor repointed and reconstructed some of the exterior brick and granite walls between 2000 and 2002. Specifically, the entire north wall was reconstructed using both historic and new brick as well as granite to match the historic. Additionally, foundation vents were installed at the top of the granite section of the north wall. As directed in the National Park Service contracting documents, all new bricks were specified to match the historic in size, shape, texture, and color and were to be molded with the year of firing, 1998, on the face of each brick. This last directive was apparently to avoid any future confusion as to which materials were original and which were the result of later modifications. Ali Miri's 1994 report illustrates that the section of the north wall beneath the bathroom window (Window 5) was filled with brick lighter in color than the surrounding materials when this area was modified and the window created between 1930- 1940. When the north wall was reconstructed between 2000 and 2002, the National Park Service contractor did not match the brick to that which existed historically in the area under Window 5, but instead matched the

FIGURE 29. View of exterior walls. Note penciling of the mortar joints.

FIGURE 30. View of southeast corner.

FIGURE 31. Flat arches typical of windows on south, east, and west elevations of main block of house.

FIGURE 32. Typical flat arch at windows on east and west ends of addition.

FIGURE 33. Cedar shingle roofing on shed-roofed addition.

FIGURE 34. Gutter and downspout at northeast corner.

remaining, older historic brick and mortar, thus mostly obliterating evidence of the earlier door.

Roofing

The main gable and shed roof of the house are finished with cedar shingle roofing. The shingles are of random sizes, measuring from 5" to 11½" wide and ½" thick with a 5" to 5½" exposure. Exposed on the interior of Rooms 104, 105, 106, 107, 108, and 109, the historic shingle lath is randomly sized from 7" to 14" wide by ½" thick. The lath is spaced at ½" to 2" apart. Some of the lath and rafters show evidence of white paint in numerous places, indicating that there was likely not a finished ceiling in the shed portion of the house originally. While it is possible that the boards were recycled from another structure when installed, no unused nail holes were observed. Some of the lath are unpainted and appear to be later replacements. Copper flashing was installed at the joint between the north wall and north shed roof. All of the cedar roofing was installed during the 2000- 2002 rehabilitation treatments completed by a National Park Service contractor.

The rafter ends are enclosed behind a simple fascia board. There is a small dentil molding at the soffit of the cornice along the south, east, and west elevations of the house.

Half round, 6" galvanized gutters are mounted at the north end of the main shed roof and the shed roof extension that covers the rear stoop. Galvanized, round downspouts measuring 4" wide are located at each end of the north elevation and at the northeast corner of the rear stoop. Additionally, half round gutters are mounted at the south end of the hipped roof. This gutter wraps the corners of the roof to the east and west and connects to round downspouts.

Chimneys

Two brick chimneys are symmetrically positioned on the north elevation of the two- story portion of the house. These chimneys are located on the north elevation of the second story of the house, at the joint with the shed rooms. Brick corbelling exists on the upper portion of the chimneys. The eastern chimney serves as the flue for the fireplaces in Rooms 103 and 104. The western chimney serves Rooms 101 and 107. Judging from the watercolors of Barnett Allen Bell, which show the chimneys to be incomplete at the tops, the top portions were rebuilt by the Bells. The chimneys are historic, but the bottom portions were repaired during the 2000 to 2002 National Park Service treatments. The new mortar and brick used matches the historic in size, color and materials.

The eastern chimney has a galvanized metal cap. Mounted to the west elevation of the western chimney is a radio antenna. The National Park Service installed this antenna as part of their communication network. In addition to the two chimneys, a metal vent pipe projects from the shed roof over the wall separating Rooms 104 and 106. Currently, nothing is associated with this pipe located in these rooms. However, it is likely a plumbing stack once associated with the bath fixtures that existed in Room 106.

FIGURE 35. Chimneys on north elevation of second story. Note that the left chimney has a galvanized metal cap.

Doors and Windows

Doors

There are eighteen historic door openings in the building. Thirteen of these openings are currently fitted with historic doors. The two entrances into the first floor of the building (Doors 1 and 7), as well as the north entrance to the basement (Doors 10), have all been fitted with new doors. Door 18, located on the east elevation of the basement wall, has been closed with a new, fixed, plywood panel. All the new doors and the fixed plywood panel were installed by the National Park Service contractor between 2000 and 2002. The historic door to the first floor bathroom (Door 9, Room 106) has been removed from the opening and is currently stored in Room 101. The historic door types in the building are primarily stile- and- rail, with the exception of Door 17, which is comprised of tongue- and- groove beaded boards.

There are three types of stile- and- rail doors in the house. Type 1 has two, long, vertical, side- by- side panels. The panels on these doors are flat and have no molding. Doors 2, 3, 4 and 5 are Type 1 and are believed to be original to the house. Type 2 has five equally- spaced panels running horizontally from the top to the bottom, with machine- molded stiles and rails. Doors 6, 8, 9, 11, 12, 13, 14, 15 and 16 are Type 2 and were likely installed by the Bell family sometime after 1930. Type 3 has four vertical panels arranged in a Latin cross configuration. The panels

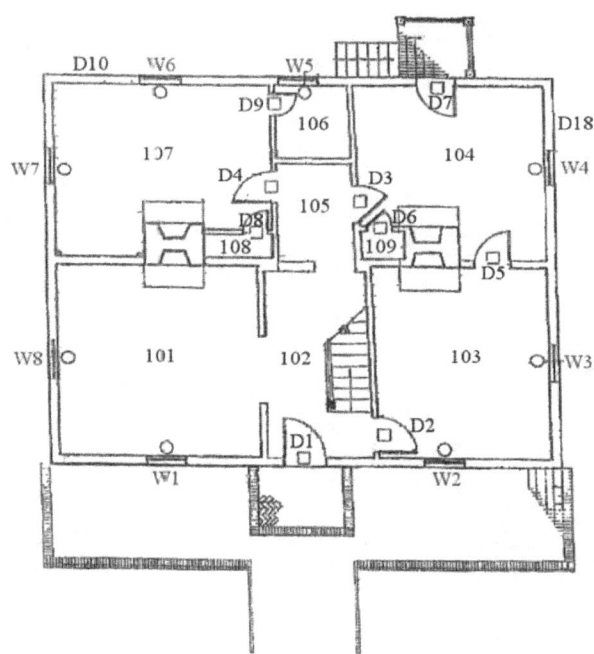

FIGURE 36. First floor plan showing door locations.

are flat and have applied molding. Doors 1 and 7 are Type 3 and are new, installed between 2000 and 2002 by the National Park Service contractor. Generally, a 5" to 5 ½" frame surrounds each of the door openings. With the exception of the newly- installed doors (Doors 1, 7, 10 and 18), all the hardware on the doors is historic. The historic hardware consists of metal butt hinges, metal

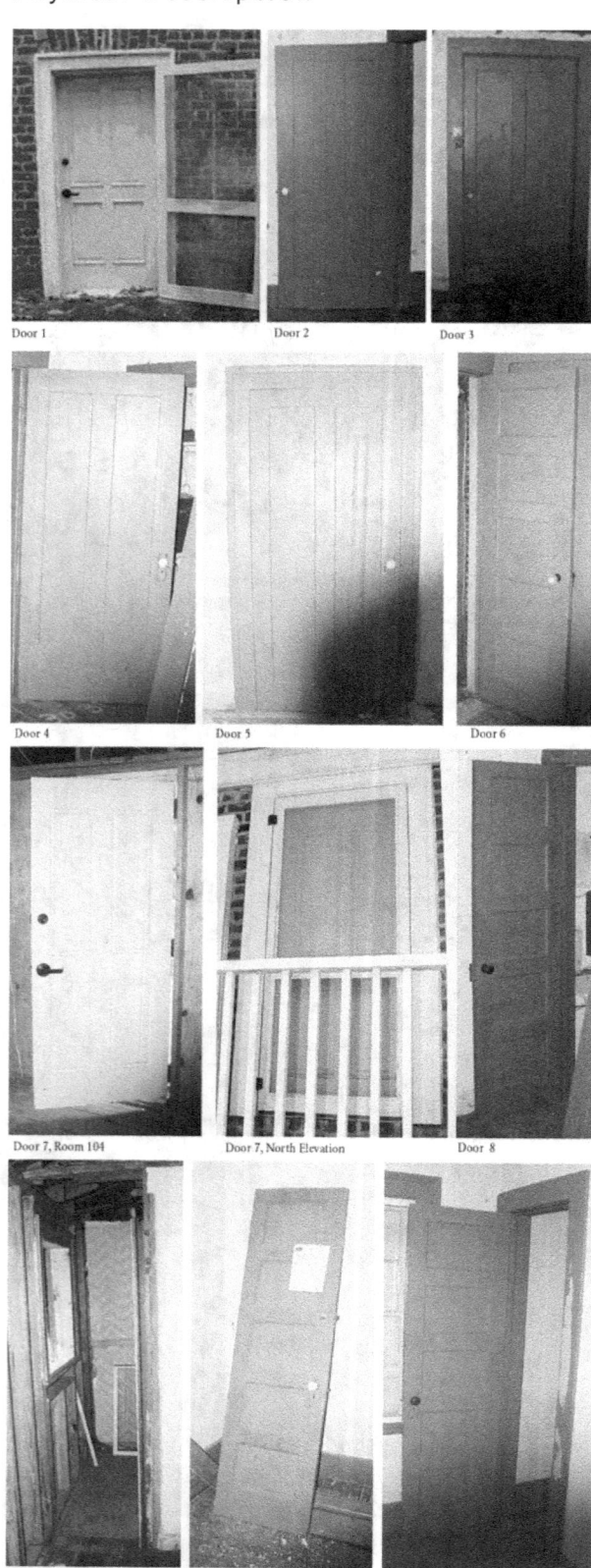

FIGURE 37. Doors 1-11.

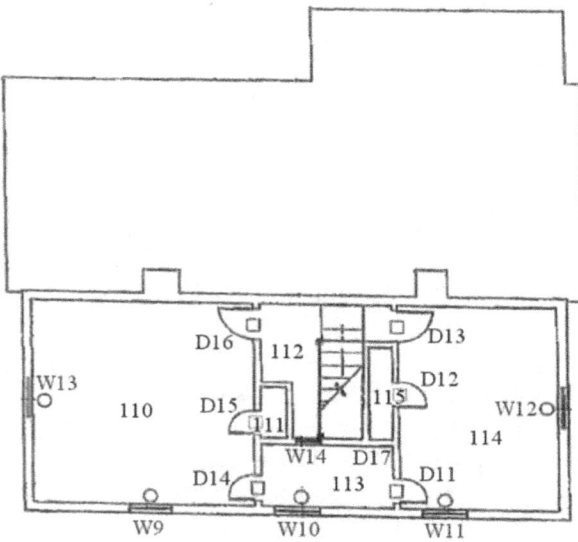

FIGURE 38. Second floor plan showing door locations.

doorknobs, (some of which are laminated), glass doorknobs, and rim- and- mortise locks. Where applicable, all of the brass plates measure 2¼" by 7" and all of the metal doorknobs measure 2½" in diameter. The glass knob measures 2" in diameter. While many of the door and hinge types are similar in size, variations are prevalent enough to warrant individual descriptions. The location, unique characteristics, and individual measurements of each of the doors are discussed on the following pages. For simplification, some of these characteristics are included in table format.

Door 1: Two doors are in this opening: a four- panel door (Type 3) and a screened door on the exterior, both of which were installed by the National Park Service contractor between 2000 and 2002. The opening is original to the building. The Type 3 door in this opening measures 2'- 11¾" by 6'- 11½" by 1¾". Applied to each of the panels is ½" molding. See details included at the end of the door descriptions. The screened door measures 3'- 0¼" by 6'- 10¾" and is comprised of two panels of wire screen framed between stiles and rails. A metal door handle is affixed to the exterior elevation of the door on the left stile. Both of the doors and the frame have been painted white. The threshold measures approximately 1'- 7" wide by 1½" thick. The hardware for this door consists of a lever- type door handle and core lock, a deadbolt, and butt hinges. The lever- type handle measures approximately 4¾" and is mounted on 3¼" base. The deadbolt lock is

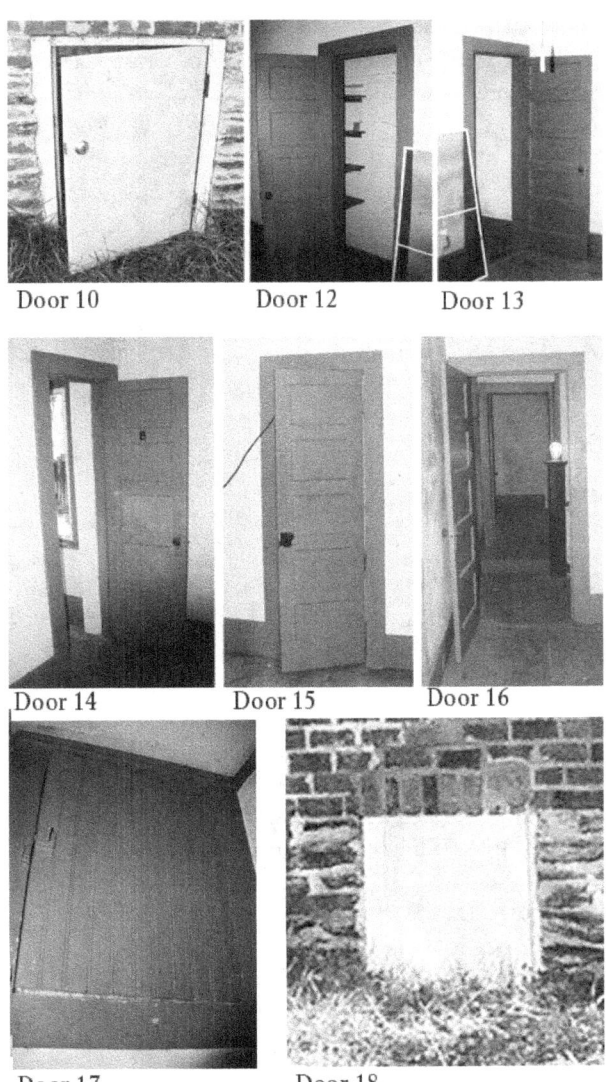

Door 10   Door 12   Door 13

Door 14   Door 15   Door 16

Door 17   Door 18

FIGURE 39. Doors 10-18.

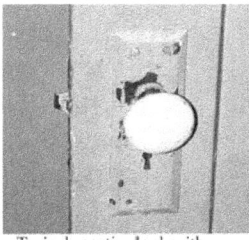

Typical mortise lock with porcelain knob

Typical rim lock with metal knob

Typical glass knob with rim lock

Modern door hardware

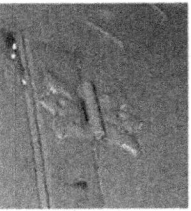

Rim lock at Door 17

Hinge at Door 17

FIGURE 40. Typcal hardware.

located just above the door handle. The butt hinges on the screen door measure 2½" by 2¾". All of the hardware is modern and was installed between 2000 and 2002 by a National Park Service contractor.

Door 2: Door 2 is Type 1 and measures 2'- 1½" by 6'-11". The opening is original to the building. Both the door and the frame are painted blue. The threshold measures 8¾" wide by ¼" to ½" thick. The hardware for this door consists of laminated metal doorknobs, a mortise lock, and butt hinges.

Door 3: Door 3 is Type 1 and measures 3'- 3" by 6'-10". The opening is original to the building. Both the door and the frame are painted blue. This door opening does not have a threshold. The hardware

for this door consists of laminated metal doorknobs, a mortise lock, and butt hinges.

Door 4: Door 4 is Type 1 and measures 3'- 0" by 6'-8¼". The opening is original to the building. Both the door and the frame have are blue. This door opening does not have a threshold. The hardware for this door consists of laminated metal doorknobs, a mortise lock, and butt hinges.

Door 5: Door 5 is Type 1 and measures 2'- 1½" by 6'-11". The opening appears to be original to the building. Both the door and the frame are painted blue. The threshold measures 8¾" wide by ¼" to ½" thick. The hardware for this door consists of laminated metal doorknobs, a mortise lock, and butt hinges.

Door 6: Door 6 is Type 2 and measures 2'- 0" by 6'- 8 ½". The opening was made by the Bell family after 1932. The western frame measures 1" wide and abuts the corner of the south and west walls. Both the door and the frame are painted blue. This door opening does rot have a threshold. The hardware for this door consists of laminated metal and glass doorknobs, a rim lock, and butt hinges.

Door 7: Door 7 is a Type 3 four- panel door with a screened door on the exterior, both of which were installed by the National Park Service contractor between 2000 and 2002. The door opening was made by the Bell family after 1932. The door in this opening measures 2'- 11" by 6'- 10" by 1¾". Applied to

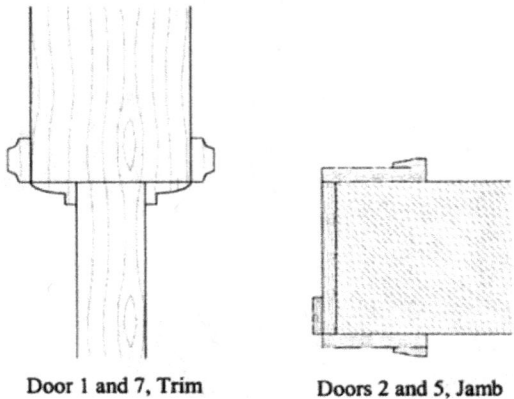

Door 1 and 7, Trim   Doors 2 and 5, Jamb

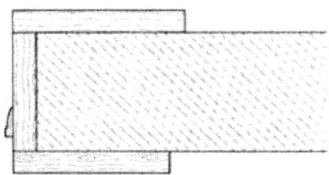

Doors 3 and 8, Jamb

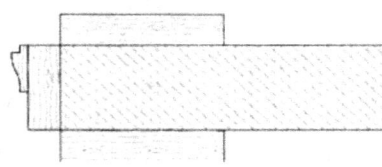

Door 4, Jamb

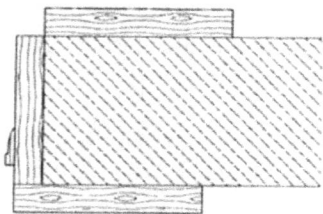

Doors 13 and 16, Jamb

FIGURE 41. Typical door jambs.

each of the panels is ½" molding. See details included at the end of the door descriptions. The screened door measures 2'- 10¾" by 6'- 10" and is comprised of two panels of wire screen framed between stiles and rails. A metal door handle is affixed to the exterior elevation of the door on the left stile. Both of the doors and the frame are painted white.

A 6¾" frame surrounds the door opening. Both the door and the frame are painted white. The threshold measures 11¾" wide by 1¾" thick. The hardware for this door consists of a lever- type door handle and core lock, a deadbolt, and butt hinges. The lever-type handle measures approximately 4¾" and is mounted on 3¼" base. The deadbolt lock is located just above the door handle. The butt hinges on the screen door measure 2½" by 2¾". This door and all the hardware is modern and was installed between 2000 and 2002 by a National Park Service contractor.

Door 8: Door 8 is Type 2 and measures 1'11½" by 6'-7¼". The door opening was made during the 1930s renovations. Both the door and the frame are painted blue. This door opening does not have a threshold. The hardware for this door consists of metal doorknobs, a rim lock, and butt hinges.

Door 9: Door 9 has been removed from its opening and is currently stored in Room 101. Door 9 is Type 2 and measures 1'11½" by 6'- 7¼". The opening for this door consists of the exposed framing. This door opening was made by the Bell family after 1932. A 5¼" by 1" piece of trim finishes this opening along the south jamb. Both the door and the trim are painted blue. This door opening does not have a threshold. The hardware for this door consists of metal doorknobs, a rim lock, and butt hinges. .

Door 10: Door 10 is flat and measures 2'- 8" by 3'- 8¾" by 1¾". Framing the opening on the left and right are two 3¾" by ¾" boards. Both the door and the frame are painted white. The hardware for this door consists of a deadbolt and butt hinges. The butt hinges measure 2½" by 2¾". This door and all of the hardware is modern and was installed between 2000 and 2002 by a National Park Service contractor.

According to photographs and drawings made of the building prior to the 2000- 2002 National Park

Table 1: Door Characteristics

Door	width	height	door type	age	hinge size	lock type
1	3'	6'-11-1/2"	4 panel	original opening new door	2-1/2 x 2-3/4	modern lever
2	3'	7'	2 panel	original	2 x 3-1/2	mortise w/ porcelain knob
3	3'-3"	6'-10"	2 panel	original	2 x 3-1/2	mortise w/ porcelain knob
4	3'	6'-9"	2 panel	original	2 x 3-1/2	mortise w/ porcelain knob
5	3'	7'	2 panel	original	2 x 3-1/2	mortise w/ porcelain knob
6	2'	6'-10"	5 panel	added after 1932	1-1/4 x 3	mortise w/ porcelain knob and glass knob
7	2'-11-1/2"	6'-10"	4 panel	opening after 1932 door replaced 2000	2-1/2 x 2-3/4	modern lever
8	1'-11-1/2"	6'-7"	5 panel	opening and door after 1932	1-3/4 x 3-1/2	metal rim lock
9	2'-2"	7'-5"	5 panel	opening and door after 1932	1-3/4 x 3-1/2	mortise w/ porcelain knob
10	1'-9-1/2"	2'-3"	5 panel	original opening new door	2 x 3-1/2	modern deadbolt
11	2'	6'-9-1/2"	5 panel	opening and door after 1932	1-1/4 x 3	mortise w/ metal knob
12	2'	6'-10"	5 panel	opening and door after 1932	1-1/4 x 3	rim lock w/ metal knob
13	2'-7-1/2"	6'-10"	5 panel	opening and door after 1932	2 x 3-1/2	mortise w/ metal knob
14	2'	6'-8"	5 panel	opening and door after 1932	1-3/4 x 3-1/2	mortise w/ metal knob
15	2'-1/2"	6'-10'	5 panel	opening and door after 1932	1-1/4 x 3	rim lock w/ metal knob
16	2'-7-1/2"	6'-10"	5 panel	opening and door after 1932	2 x 3-1/2	rim lock w/ metal knob
17	1'-5-3/4"	2'	tongue-and-groove	opening and door after 1932	2-1/2	rim lock w/ metal knob
18	2'-3-1/2"	2'-3"	plywood panel	original opening new door	n/a	n/a

Service stabilization treatments, this door was originally of board- and- batten construction and had strap hinges.

Door 11: Door 11 is Type 2 and measures 2'- 0" by 6'-8½". The door opening was made by the Bell family after 1932. Both the door and the frame are painted blue. This door opening does not have a threshold. The hardware for this door consists of metal doorknobs, a mortise lock, and butt hinges.

Door 12: Door 12 is Type 2 and measures 2'- 0" by 6'-8½". The door opening was made by the Bell family after 1932. Both the door and the frame are painted blue. This door opening does not have a threshold. The hardware for this door consists of metal doorknobs, a mortise lock, and butt hinges.

Door 13: Door 13 is Type 2 and measures 2'- 7¾" by 6'- 8". The door opening was made by the Bell

family after 1932. Both the door and the frame are painted blue. The threshold measures 5½" by ¾". The hardware for this door consists of metal doorknobs, a mortise lock, and butt hinges.

Door 14: Door 14 is Type 2 and measures 2'- 0" by 6'-8 ½". The door opening was made by the Bell family after 1932. Both the door and the frame are painted blue. This door opening does not have a threshold. The hardware for this door consists of metal doorknobs, a mortise lock, and butt hinges.

Door 15: Door 15 is Type 2 and measures 2'- 0" by 6'-8 ½". The door opening was made by the Bell family after 1932. Both the door and the frame are painted blue. This door opening does not have a threshold. The hardware for this door consists of metal doorknobs, a mortise lock, and butt hinges.

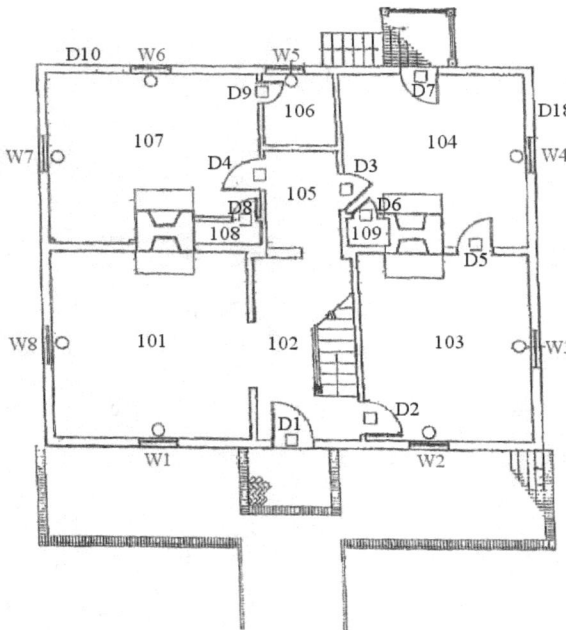

FIGURE 42. First floor window openings.

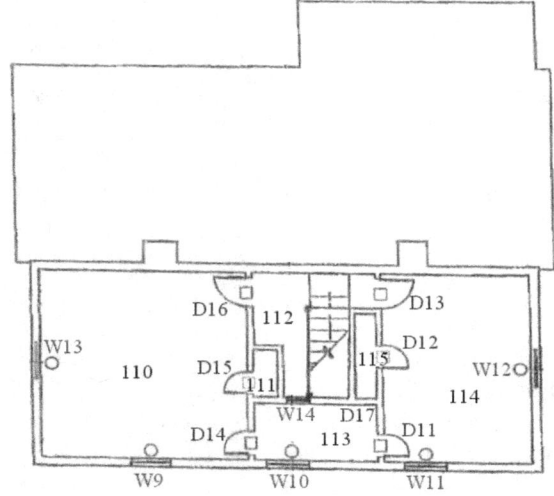

FIGURE 43. Second floor window openings.

Door 16: Door 16 is Type 2 and measures 2'- 7¾" by 6'- 8". The door opening was made by the Bell family after 1932. Both the door and the frame are painted blue. The threshold measures 5½" by ¾". The hardware for this door consists of metal doorknobs, a mortise lock, and butt hinges. See photographs on the following pages.

Door 17: Door 17 is located on the upper portion of the north wall of Room 113 and provides access to the attic. The door opening was made by the Bell family after 1932. The door measures 1'- 5¾" by 2'- 0"

and is comprised of six, tongue- and- groove, beaded boards, five of which measure 3¼" wide. The sixth board measures 1½". A 4½" frame surrounds the opening. Both the door and the frame are painted blue. The hardware on this door consists of a metal rim lock with a thumb turn latch and decorative butt hinges that measure 2½" by 1¾". See photographs on the following pages.

Door 18: The historic door for this opening has been removed. A 1'- 8" by 2'- 3" by ¾" plywood panel has been installed in the opening, framed on either side with 3¾" by ¾" plywood trim. Both the door and the frame are painted white. According to photographs and drawings made of the building prior to the 2000- 2002 National Park Service stabilization treatments, this door was originally of board- and- batten construction.

Windows

There are fourteen windows in Allenbrook. All but one of these windows have double- hung sashes, each with six divided lights. Window 14, located in the wall dividing Room 112, the upstairs hall, and Room 113, the upstairs bath, is a fixed, single- light window. Window openings 1, 2, 3, 4, 6, 7, 8, 9, 10, 11, 12, and 13 appear to be original to the house. According to photographs included in Ali Miri's 1994 report, Window 5 was installed in place of an original door, evidenced by the brick patching in the north wall beneath the window. The handwritten note from Barnett Bell, included in Miri's report, confirms this observation and dates this window to after 1932. Likewise, Window 14 was added by the Bell family after 1932, when the upstairs loft was subdivided into rooms. Ali Miri's report also indicates a window was originally located on the north elevation of the house where Door 7 currently exists.

The original window openings are larger in size than those added later. Typically, the window openings measure 2'- 11" by 4'- 5½" and are finished with 5" wide trim along the top and two sides. The general overall measurements of the windowsills are 1'- 0¾" by 3'- 11" by 1½". A 3" by ½" stool is attached to the top of the sill on the interior of the opening. The sashes measure 2'- 10½" by 2'- 3½". The muntins in each sash are molded and measure 1" wide by ¾" thick. Windows 5, 6, and 14 have unique measurements. See the individual descriptions for details.

Several of the windows have one or more broken panes. All of the window sashes are painted white and, on the interior, the trim is also painted white. The National Park Service installed new hardware on the historic sashes and interior storm windows in the historic openings, likely to provide for security and insulation. Tongue- and- groove, board- and-batten shutters are mounted on the exterior of each of the windows except at Window 14, which is an interior window. The shutters are comprised of eight boards, each measuring between 1¼" to 2½" wide and ¾" thick. Overall, a shutter measures approximately 1'- 5" wide by 4'- 5" tall. The exterior trim around the windows typically measures 1¾" wide by 1¼" thick. Both the exterior trim and the shutters have been painted white. The National Park Service contractor installed new strap hinges and slide bolts on all the shutters. New shutter dogs have also been mounted to the exterior brick wall surface on either side of the exterior windows. The locations of the windows are detailed on the floor plan below. Where unique, the window characteristics are discussed on the following pages.

Window 1: This window opening is typical. At the initial investigation, two center panes in each of the sashes were shattered. More panes have been lost since.

Window 2: This window opening is typical. All the windowpanes in the two sashes have been shattered.

Window 3 This window opening is typical. All the windowpanes in this window are intact.

Window 4: This window opening is typical. All the windowpanes in the two sashes have been shattered. A sash stay is located approximately halfway up the north jamb of the window. The stay is wood and measures approximately 1" by 3" by 1".

Window 5: Window opening 5 measures 2'- 8" by 3'-0". The opening is finished with trim along the top and sides, measuring 3½" and 5" wide, respectively. A new sill has been installed, which measures 7¾" by 2'- 8". A new head and jamb have also been installed. The National Park Service contractor installed the new materials in this window. The sashes measure 2'- 7½" by 1'- 6¾". The muntins in each sash measure 1" wide by ¾" thick. All the windowpanes in this window are intact.

Window 1, exterior and interior

Window 2, exterior and interior

Window 3, exterior and interior

Window 4   Window 5

FIGURE 44. Windows 1-5.

Window 6, exterior and interior

Window 7, exterior and interior

Window 8, exterior and interior

Window 9, exterior and interior

FIGURE 45. Windows 6-9.

This window was added to the house during the 1930s renovations of the house.

Window 6: Window opening 6 measures 2'-11" by 4'-4". The opening is finished with trim along the top and sides, measuring 6" and 5" wide, respectively. A 1'-5½" by 3'-11" by 1½" sill finishes the opening. The sashes measure 2'-10½" by 2'-3". The muntins in each sash measure 1" wide by ¾" thick. The National Park Service contractor installed a new head and jamb in this window. All the windowpanes in this window are intact.

Window 7: This window opening is typical. All the windowpanes in this window are intact.

Window 8: This window opening is typical. All the windowpanes in this window are intact.

Window 9 This window opening is typical. One of the windowpanes in the lower sash is shattered.

Window 10: This window opening is typical. Two of the windowpanes in both the upper and lower sashes are shattered.

Window 11: This window opening is typical. One of the windowpanes in the upper sash and two in the lower sash are shattered.

Window 12: This window opening is typical. All the windowpanes in this window are intact.

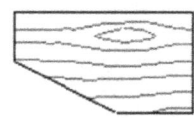

Typical Backband, Window 1

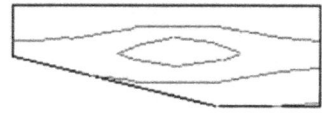

Typical backband, Windows 6 & 7

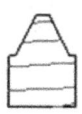

Typical muntin profile

FIGURE 46. Window details.

Window 13: This window opening is typical. All the windowpanes in this window are intact.

Window 14: Window 14 is a fixed, single-pane window located on the wall separating Room 113, the upstairs bath, and Room 112, the upstairs hall. This window was added during the 1930s renovations. The windowpane measures 2'-1" by 1'-5". The window is finished with trim measuring 5" by 3'-0½" by ¾" along the top and bottom and 5" by 1'-6¾" by ¾" along the sides. A ¾" molding frames the interior edges of the trim.

Interior Finish Materials and Characteristics

Several of the interior finishes are similar throughout the first and second floors of the house. All of the floorboards are tongue-and-groove and measure 11" to 11¼" wide by 1" thick and run east to west. Upon inspection, no saw marks were evident. It appears the floorboards are planed and original to the house.

Paint

All of the walls and ceilings, where present, are painted white. The crown and base molding, window casings, and doors are all painted blue. Likewise, the fireplace mantels in Rooms 101, 103 and 104 are painted blue. The mantel in Room 107 is unpainted. The brick chimneybreasts and fireboxes in all four of the fireplaces are painted black. The stairs leading from Room 102 to Room 112 are painted blue, the balusters and newel posts are painted white, and the handrail is stained dark brown.

Basement

The house has a partial basement at the north side that extends to a shallow crawl space along the south side. As discussed in the Structural Systems section of this report, the walls of the basement are concrete block, constructed by a National Park Service contractor between 2000 and 2002. The basement floor is poured concrete. A metal drainage grate is in the floor near the basement stairs. As noted in Ali Miri's 1994 report, the floor of the basement was originally clay. It is presumed the existing floor was laid during the 2000-2002 stabilization of the house.

Window 10, exterior and interior

Window 12, exterior and interior

Window 13, exterior and interior

Window 14, interior   Window 11, interior

FIGURE 47. Windows 10-14.

FIGURE 48. Grate in basement floor.

FIGURE 49. Arched opening in east wall of Room 101.

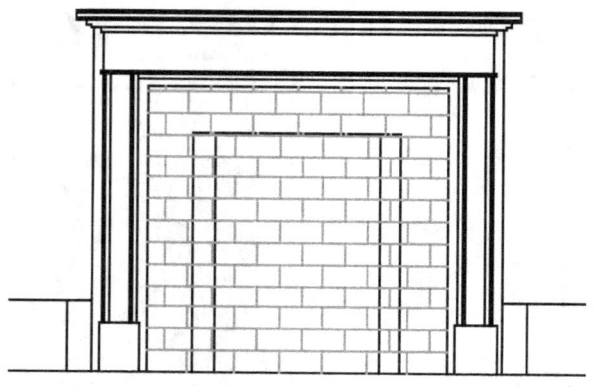

FIGURE 50. Fireplace in Room 101.

Room 101 / Living Room

Room 101 is in the southwest corner of the house, on the first floor. The overall measurements of this room are 16'- 4" by 16'- 7". The room is accessed via the central hall, Room 102, through an arched opening in its east wall. There are no doors in this opening. According to the handwritten note by Barnett Bell, the archway was added to the house by the Bell family. The overall measurements of the opening are 5'- 11½" by 6'- 10¼" by 5½". Door 9, which is marked as belonging to the first floor bathroom, Room 106, is propped against the north wall to the west of the fireplace.

Ceiling. The height of the ceiling in Room 101 is 8'-8½" above the finished floor. Water damage is evident in various areas of the ceiling.

Walls. The walls are plaster on lath and finished with white paint. The lath measures approximately 1½" wide by ¼" thick. Water damage is evident on various areas of the walls throughout the room.

Trim. Molding measuring 3½" by 3" crowns the walls. The baseboards along the walls in this room are 9½" wide. There are 1" quarter- round moldings along bottom of the baseboards. The quarter- round moldings are unfinished. All the crown and base molding was added during the 1930s renovations of the house.

Fireplace. Located on the north wall is a brick fireplace with a mantelpiece measuring 5'- 5" wide. Overall, the fireplace is 4'- 11¾" wide and 4'- 5½" tall above the finished floor. The firebox measures 2'- 6" wide. Separating the mantel piece and the firebox is a header that measures 7¾" wide. Flanking the firebox is pilaster- like detailing. The hearth is fieldstone and measures 4'- 9" wide. According to a handwritten note by Barnett A. Bell, the mantel is made of pine and was added, along with the fieldstone hearth, to the house by the Bell family.

Electrical and Heating and Cooling Fixtures.
Exposed wiring is located on either side of the opening to Room 101, on the east wall. This wiring likely provided electrical service to wall sconces at one point. A track is mounted to the ceiling that once held track lighting. Other electrical fixtures in this room include a duplex outlet in the baseboard of the east wall, two three- pronged outlets in the baseboards of the south and west walls, and a

security system motion sensor in the southeast corner of the room.

The heating and cooling fixtures include a 1'- 3½" by 1'- 1½" return vent in the floorboards, located approximately 1"from the north wall, just east of the fireplace, and two supply vents. One vent is located approximately 11" from the west wall and measures 1'- 3¼" by 5½". The other vent is located approximately 1½" off the south wall and measures 2'- 8" by 10".

Room 102

Room 102 is the central hall on the first floor. The staircase leading to the second floor is located along the east wall in this room. The overall measurements of this room are 8'- 3½" by 16'- 1".

Ceiling. The height of the ceiling in Room 102 is 8'-9½". The ceiling is plaster on lath. Severe water damage is evident on a portion of the ceiling near the arched opening to Room 101 to the west. The ceiling at the base of the stairs is angled. It is presumed that this was a post- 1932 modification to the ceiling to accommodate plumbing for the second story bathroom located above the southern end of the first floor hall.

Flooring. Along the west wall, just north of the arched opening to Room 101, very faint remnants of a painted floor cloth can be seen. Historic documents indicate that the Roswell Historical Society painted this floor cloth during their occupation of the building in the late 1980s. At the north end of the hall, a faint shadow exists on the floorboards. This shadow may be indicative of an earlier door at this location.

Staircase. A staircase leading to the second floor is located along the east wall of the hall. The height of the staircase from the finished floor of Room 102 to the underside of the top landing is 7'- 5". The stairs are comprised of nine 12" by 3'- 3" by 1¼" treads and eleven 8" risers. At the base of the stairs is a shallow tread measuring 12" by 3'- 9" by 1¼" and, at the top of the stairs, immediately before the landing, is a 10½" by 3'- 3" by 1¼" tread. A balustrade comprised of fifteen 1" square balusters, a 2½" by 3" hand rail, a 4'- 4¼" tall, ornamental newel post at the base and a 4'- 1½" tall simple newel post at the top encloses the stairs to the west. The risers and treads of the staircase are painted blue. The balusters and the

FIGURE 51. Fireplace in Room 101.

FIGURE 52. View of staircase in Room 102.

FIGURE 53. Baseboard on north wall of Room 102. Note that right end is plaster.

FIGURE 54. Beaded-board paneling on underside of staircase.

FIGURE 55. Water-damaged ceiling in Room 102.

newel post at the bottom of the stairs are painted white, and the handrail and the newel post at the top of the stairs are stained a dark color, possibly walnut. According to the handwritten note by Barnett Bell, the staircase was added by the Bell family, and the newel post at the base of the stairs was recycled from the Glades Plantation and is of circa 1840 vintage. The underside of the stairs is finished with horizontally- installed beaded boards measuring 3¼" wide with two ¼" beads per board. The boards span two stringers. The beaded board finish is painted white.

Walls. The walls are plaster on lath. The lath measures approximately 1½" wide by ¼" thick. A portion of the east wall near the lower steps in the staircase was opened to install plumbing during the post- 1932 renovations undertaken by the Bell family. This area of the wall was patched with gypsum board, a portion of which has been removed, exposing the lath. Beneath the staircase on the east wall is the finished backside of the built- in- case located in the west wall of Room 103. The back of the case is finished with horizontally- installed beaded boards. The boards measure 3¼" wide, each having two ¼" beads. The beaded boards are framed on the left with 1¼" wide trim and on the right side with ¾" wide trim. The case was added to the house by the Bell family.

Trim. Molding measuring 2" by 2½" crowns the walls. Baseboards measuring 9½" to 10½" wide finish each of the walls in this room. There are 1" quarter- round moldings along the bottom of the baseboards. The quarter- round moldings are unfinished. The molding was added to the house by the Bell family.

Electrical and Heating and Cooling Fixtures. There are no light fixtures in the hall. However, a switch plate is mounted on the west wall. A three- pronged outlet is mounted on the baseboard of the east wall beneath the staircase. Another three- pronged outlet is mounted on the baseboard of the west wall. Electrical wiring conduit is located in the north corner of the west wall. A smoke detector is mounted on the ceiling. The only heating and cooling fixture in the hall is a 10½" by 1'- 1¾" supply vent located approximately 1" from the southern end of the west wall.

Room 103 / Dining Room

Room 103 is in the southeast corner of the house, on the first floor. The overall measurements of this room are 14'- 0½" by 16'- 7". The room is accessed from the central hall, Room 102, through Door 2, located in its western wall near the southeast corner.

Ceiling.   The height of the ceiling in Room 103 is 9'-1½" to 9'- 3" above the finished floor. The ceiling is newer gypsum board and was apparently installed by the Roswell Historical Society circa 1980s.

Walls. The walls are plaster on lath and finished with white paint. The lath measures approximately 1½" wide by ¼" thick. A built- in- case in the west wall measures 2'- 7½" by 6'- 0" by 5". Five shelves line the case, each measuring 1'- 9½" by 5" by ¾". The head and jamb of the case are 5" wide. A 4" by ¼" trim lines the head and jamb on the interior of the case. A 2½" quarter- round trim frames the case. This case was installed by the Bell family in the location of a former door opening sometime after 1932.

Trim.   .Molding measuring 3½" by 3" crowns the walls. Baseboards finish each of the walls in this room. All the crown and base molding was added to the house by the Bell family. The finish characteristics on the north wall include trim 10¼" wide to the east of fireplace and 7½" wide to the west. There is 1" quarter- round trim molding along the bottom of the east baseboard on this wall, and the molding is unfinished. On the east, north and west walls, the trim is 7½" to 8" wide with 1" quarter- round shoe molding. The molding is unfinished.

Fireplace.   Located on the north wall is a brick fireplace with a wood mantelpiece, measuring 5" by 5'- 9" by 1½". Overall, the fireplace is 5'- 2½" wide and 4'- 5½" tall above the finished floor. The firebox measures 2'- 6" wide. Separating the mantel piece and the firebox is a detailed header that measures 7¾" wide. Flanking the firebox is pilaster- like detailing. The hearth is fieldstone and measures 4'-10" wide. The mantel is similar to that located in Room 101, which was added to the house, along with the fieldstone hearth, by the Bell family. Though not so documented, it is reasonable to assume that this mantel and hearth were also added by the Bells.

Electrical and Heating and Cooling Fixtures.   One light fixture is mounted on a track on the ceiling. A

FIGURE 56. Bui t-in case on west wall of Room 103.

FIGURE 57. Flooring in Room 103.

duplex outlet is mounted on the baseboard of the west wall, two three- pronged outlets are mounted on the baseboard of the east wall, and one three- pronged outle: and a phone jack are mounted on the baseboard of the south wall. Additionally, a thermostat and a security system motion sensor are mounted on the west wall. Electrical wiring is exposed in the built- in- case in the west wall and just south of the case. The heating and cooling fixtures include a 1'- 3¾" by 1'- 1¾" return vent in the

FIGURE 58. Flooring in Room 104.

FIGURE 59. Doors 5, 6, &, 7 in Room 104.

FIGURE 60. Fireplace in Room 104.

floorboards located approximately 5" from the west wall, in the northwest corner, as well as two supply vents. One vent is located approximately 9" from the east wall and measures 1'-3½" by 5½". The other vent is located flush against the baseboard of the south wall and measures 2'-8" by 10".

Room 104 / Kitchen

Room 104 is in the northeast corner of the house, on the first floor. The overall measurements of this room are 14'-10" by 14'-10".

Ceiling. There is no finished ceiling in this room, so the shed roof framing and roofing materials are exposed to the room. The height to the top of the north wall beam is 7'-9" and to the top of the south wall beam is 13'-6".

Flooring. The flooring is typical throughout this room except for a few boards that measure 8" and 9" in width.

Walls. The south, east, and west walls are plaster on lath. The lath measures approximately 1½" wide by ¼" thick. A portion of the plaster is removed along the northern end of the east wall, revealing the exterior brick wall underneath. A portion of the west wall is opened to expose interior plumbing, likely installed for the adjacent former bathroom, Room 106. The north wall was reconstructed by the National Park Service contractor and is exposed framing. The wall structure is comprised of 1½" by 3¾" studs, measuring 7'-3" tall and spaced at 16" on center. The top plate is comprised of two sistered 1½" by 3½" boards, and the sill is a single 1½" by 3½" beam. Plywood sheathing is exposed to the room.

Trim. Flat molding measuring 5½" with a ¼" bead and a 1" quarter-round trim along the bottom crowns the south, east, and west walls. This molding was added to the house by the Bell family, sometime after 1932.

Fireplace. Located on the south wall is a brick fireplace with a wood mantelpiece. Overall, the fireplace is 5'-1½" wide and 4'-7" tall above the finished floor. The firebox measures 2'-9" wide by 2'-8½" tall by 1'-3" deep. The mantel shelf measures 10½" by 5'-10½" by 1". Separating the mantel shelf and the firebox is a detailed header that, overall, measures approximately 5'-1½" wide by 12½" tall. Flanking the firebox are the sides of the mantelpiece, which measure approximately 10" wide by 3'- 7½". The hearth is 4'- 9" wide. This mantel is similar to that located in Room 107, which, according to a handwritten note by Barnett A. Bell, is heart- pine and original to the house. It is reasonable to assume that this mantel is also original. The fieldstone hearth was added to the house by the Bell family sometime after 1932.

Electrical and Heating and Cooling Fixtures. There is a mounting for a fluorescent light fixture on the west wall, 7¾" north of Door 3. The fixture measures 3" by 4'- 0" by 1½". According to a photograph included in Ali Miri's 1994 report, this fixture held task lighting. Other electrical fixtures in this room include: two duplex outlets on the west wall, north of Door 3; exposed sconce wiring on the east wall west of Door 4; a light switch for the exterior light outside Door 7 on the north wall; a smoke detector mounted on a rafter in the southwest corner of the room; and a security system motion detector in the southwest corner of the room, over Door 3. Additionally, an electrical breaker box is mounted to the southern end of the east wall.

The heating and cooling fixtures include two supply vents measuring 5½" by 1'- 3". One is located 5" from the east wall beneath Window 4 and the other is located 5½" from the north wall, east of Door 7.

Room 105

Room 105 is centrally located north of Room 102, on the first floor. The overall measurements of this room are 6'- 1" by 8'- 8".

Ceiling. There is no finished ceiling in this room, so the shed roof framing and roofing materials are exposed to the room. It appears that a lowered ceiling once existed in this room, as is evidenced by the truncated walls.

Walls. The walls do not extend all the way to the underside of the roof in this room. The ceiling that formerly existed in this room rested on the tops of the walls, creating an attic space above. The walls are 7'- 7½" tall. The east, north, and west walls are plaster on lath and date to the post- 1932 renovation work completed by the Bell family. The south wall, above the doorway, is exposed brick.

Electrical and Heating and Cooling Fixtures. An ADT security system code pad is mounted on the

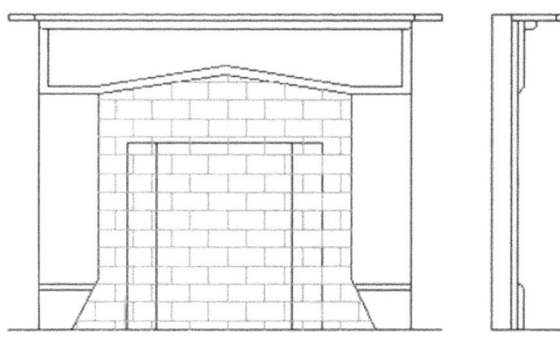

FIGURE 61. Mantel in Room 104.

FIGURE 62. View of upper portion of east and south walls in Room 105 and exposed roof framing above.

FIGURE 63. Detail of truncated west wall in Room 105, looking towards Room 107.

FIGURE 64. East wall in Room 106.

FIGURE 65. Southeastern view in Room 107.

southern end of the west wall. It appears to be functioning. A damaged thermostat is mounted on the north jamb of Door 3, in the east wall.

Room 106 / Bathroom

Room 106 is centrally located north of Room 105, on the first floor. The overall measurements of this room are 6'- 0" by 5'- 10". This room was formerly used as a bathroom, though it currently does not contain plumbing fixtures. The contractor for the National Park Service removed the plumbing fixtures during the 2000- 2002 stabilization projects. The plumbing stack still exists on the outside of the building.

Ceiling. There is no finished ceiling in this room, so the shed roof framing and roofing materials are exposed in the room. A lowered ceiling once existed in this room, as evidenced by the truncated east, south, and west walls.

Flooring. The flooring is plywood, probably installed by the National Park Service upon removal of the plumbing fixtures.

Walls. The south, east, and west walls are plasterboard applied over lath. Wallpaper finishes the walls. The north wall has been reconstructed by the National Park Service contractor and is exposed framing. The wall structure is comprised of 1½" by 3¾" studs, measuring 7'- 3" tall and spaced at 16" on center. The top plate is comprised of two sistered 1½" by 3½" boards, and the sill is a single 1½" by 3½" beam. Plywood sheathing is exposed to the room.

Electrical and Heating and Cooling Fixtures. A switch plate and a three- pronged outlet are located on the west wall.

Room 107 / Sitting Room

Room 107 is in the northwest corner of the house, on the first floor. The overall measurements of this room are 17'- 6" by 14'- 8½"

Ceiling. There is no finished ceiling in this room, so the shed roof framing and roofing materials are exposed to the room. The height to the top of the north wall beam is 7'- 6" and to the top of the south wall beam is 13'- 1". A lowered ceiling once existed in this room, evidenced by the truncated east and south walls and by the shadow lines of crown molding visible approximately two-thirds of the way up the wall.

Flooring. The flooring is typical throughout this room except for a few boards that measure 8" and 9" in width.

Walls and Trim. The wall characteristics are the same as those identified in Room 104. However, in Room 107, there are shadow lines of wall molding that existed on the south and west walls. This molding ran horizontally just above window level, finished the southwest corner of the room, and also ran along the base of the walls. Stacks of blue molding are piled against the south wall of this room. It is presumed that this is the molding that once finished the walls.

Fireplace. Located on the south wall is a brick fireplace with a wood mantelpiece. Overall, the fireplace is 4'-11" wide and 4'-5" tall above the finished floor. The firebox measures 2'-9" wide by 2'-8½" tall by 1'-3" deep. The mantel shelf measures 10" by 5'-9" by 1". Separating the mantel shelf and the firebox is a detailed header that, overall, measures approximately 4'-11" wide by 12½" tall. Flanking the firebox are the sides of the mantelpiece, which measure approximately 10" wide by 3'-7½". The hearth is 4'-11" wide. According to the 1957 newspaper article about Allenbrook, the mantel is heart-pine and original to the house. The fieldstone hearth was added to the house by the Bell family, sometime after 1932.

Electrical and Heating and Cooling Fixtures. There are two duplex outlets in this room: one is on the east wall, and the other is on the west wall beneath Window 7. A light fixture and electrical wiring conduit are mounted to the rafters in the roof structure. The heating and cooling fixtures include two supply vents measuring 5½" by 1'-3" and one return vent measuring 1'-4" square. The supply vents are located 3½" from the west wall beneath Window 7 and ½" from the north wall beneath Window 6. The return vent is located 4½" from the western end of the south wall.

Room 108

Located in the southeast corner of Room 107 is a closet, Room 108. The overall measurements of the closet are 5'-7" by 2'-0".

FIGURE 66. View of Room 107, looking west.

FIGURE 67. Fireplace in Room 107.

FIGURE 68. View of exposed roof framing in Room 107.

FIGURE 69. View of closet 108.

Ceiling. There is no finished ceiling in this room, so the shed roof framing and roofing materials are exposed in the room. A lowered ceiling once existed in this room, evidenced by the truncated east and north walls.

Flooring. The flooring is plywood, probably installed by the National Park Service during the 2000- 2002 rehabilitation projects.

Walls . The walls are plasterboard. Shelves line the south and west walls of the closet. On the south wall are a shelf and a clothes hanging bar. The shelf measures 11½" by 4'- 8" by ¾". On the west wall are three shelves that measure, from top to bottom, 1'- 2" by 2'- 0" by ¾", 1'- 4" by 2'- 0" by ¾", and 1'- 6" by 2'- 0" by ¾".

Electrical and Heating and Cooling Fixtures. A switch plate and light socket are mounted on the

north wall. An ADT central monitoring security system is mounted on the east wall of the closet. It appears to be functioning.

Room 109

Located in the southwest corner of Room 104 is a closet, Room 109. The overall measurements of the closet are 3'- 3" by 2'- 5½".

Ceiling. The ceiling is plaster on lath. The ceiling is attached to the underside of the roof rafters and follows the pitch of the roof, so the height varies.

Flooring. Wood subflooring is exposed in the closet. It is covered by the remnants of patterned linoleum, which has been laid across the floor and 2" up the side of the west wall.

Walls. The west wall is the exposed framing and plaster on lath that is the back of the finished wall in Rooms 105. Sash- sawn framing in this wall indicates it is likely part of the original construction. The east, north and south walls are plasterboard. Shelf brackets line the north, east, and south walls of the closet. These brackets are boards nailed to the walls and currently do not support any shelving. On the east wall, there are two brackets that measure 1¾" by 2¾" by 2'- 8½". On the south wall there is a set of two brackets and a set of three brackets, divided by a 1¾" by 2" board. The set of two brackets measures 1¾" by 2¾" by 2'- 8½". The set of three brackets measures ¾" by 2¼" by 1'- 2¼". On the north wall, there are three brackets, each measuring 2¼ by ¾" by 11'. The shelf measures 11½" by 4'- 8" by ¾". On the west wall there are three shelves that measure, from top to bottom, 1'- 2" by 2'- 0" by ¾", 1'- 4" by 2'- 0" by ¾" and 1'- 6" by 2'- 0" by ¾".

Electrical and Heating and Cooling Fixtures. Exposed wiring and a light socket are located on the west wall.

Room 110

All interior walls and windows, most wall coverings, all doors, and electrical and plumbing fixtures on the second floor date to the renovations completed by the Bell family in the 1930s. Only the flooring, exterior walls and windows, and roof structure of the upper level are original to the building. However, all these features are historic. Modifications made by the Roswell Historical Society in the 1980s are noted and are non- historic.

Room 110 is in the southwest corner of the house, on the second floor. The overall measurements of this room are 16'- 9" by 16'- 2". The National Park Service currently uses this room to house a communications radio.

Ceiling. The height of the ceiling in Room 110 is 10'- 0½" above the finished floor. The ceiling is plaster and is painted white.

Walls. The walls are plaster on lath. The lath measures approximately 1½" wide by ¼" thick.

Trim. Molding measuring 2" crowns the walls. Baseboards measuring 10" wide with a 1" quarter-round trim finish each of the walls in this room.

Electrical and Heating and Cooling Fixtures. Two fluorescent light fixtures are mounted on the ceiling. Additionally, one decorative cast iron sconce is mounted to the east wall south of Door 16. Six duplex outlets are mounted to the baseboards in this room: two on the north and west walls and one on the south and east walls. The outlet on the east wall is located just above the baseboard. The heating and cooling fixtures include two supply vents in the ceiling, along the north and south walls.

Room 111

Located on the east wall of Room 110 is a closet, Room 111. The overall measurements of the closet are 1'- 9¼" by 4'- 0½".

Ceiling. The ceiling is beaded board running north to south. Each board measures 3¼" wide with two ¼" beads. A square opening in the ceiling provides very limited access to the attic.

Walls. The walls are finished with beaded board. The boards are horizontally installed and measure 3¼" wide with two ¼" beads. One 8½" wide shelf supported by a 3¼" wide bracket is mounted on the north wall of the closet.

Electrical and Heating and Cooling Fixtures. A ceramic light socket is mounted on the west wall of the closet, north of Door 15.

Room 112

Located just beyond the top stair landing is the second floor hall. The landing measures 2'- 4½" by 3'- 3". There is ¾" quarter- round molding framing

FIGURE 70. Flooring in Room 110.

FIGURE 71. Sconce mounted on east wall in Room 110.

FIGURE 72. View to hall from Room 110.

FIGURE 73. South wall of Room 112. Note Window 14, which opens to bathroom.

FIGURE 74. Over view of landing at top of stairs in Room 112.

the north, east, and west sides of the landing. From the landing is a step up on either side to the hall floor, which leads to Rooms 110 to the west and Room 114 to the east. The risers in the landing steps measure 8¾" by 3'- 2". The measurement of the tread outside Room 114 is 2'- 4¾" by 2'- 5½". The

overall measurements of the hall to the west of the landing are 4'- 10¼" by 11'- 0". The hall narrows towards the south at a point approximately 6'- 7" from the north wall. The hall from this point to the southern wall is 1'- 8" by 4'- 6½" wide.

Ceiling. The ceiling is plaster.

Flooring. The flooring is comprised of a random arrangement of 6½" to 11¼" tongue- and- groove boards running east to west. The floorboards are unfinished. There is ¾" quarter- round molding at the joint between the treads and risers at the steps from the landing.

Walls. The north wall is plaster on lath. While they appear to be finished with plaster, it is unknown if the east, west and south walls are plasterboard or are plaster on lath due to lack of access to the interior framing. Window 14, which leads to Room 113, is located in the south wall.

Trim. There is ¾" quarter- round molding at the base of the walls.

Balustrade at Staircase. Framing the stairwell to the west is a balustrade spanning from the top newel post to the south wall of the hall. The balustrade is comprised of twenty- one 2'- 5½" by 1¼" by 1" balusters spaced at approximately 4½" to 5½" on center. A 2'- 11½" by 3" square newel post is located at the end of the balustrade at the south wall. A 2½" by 3" handrail spans the newel posts and balusters. The balusters are painted white, and the newel posts and handrail are stained a dark color, possibly walnut.

Electrical and Heating and Cooling Fixtures. A single bulb light is mounted to the newel post at the top of the stairs. This fixture has a ceramic casing over it.

Room 113
Located between Rooms 110 and 114 on the south side of the house is a bathroom. The overall measurements of this room are 9'- 11" by 4'- 9".

Ceiling. The height of the ceiling is 10'- 1" above the finished floor. The ceiling is plaster.

Walls. The south wall is plaster on lath. While they appear to be finished with plaster, it is unknown if the east, west, and north walls are plasterboard or plaster on lath due to lack of access to the interior framing.

Trim. A 3" by 1" chair rail molding is located on the north wall, 4'-1¾" above the finished floor. A 9½" baseboard with 1¾" trim and 1" quarter- round molding is along the south wall.

Bathroom Fixtures. A free- standing, ball- foot bathtub, a toilet, and a wall- mounted sink are located along the north wall of this room. The tub appears to retain its original fixtures. Above the sink is a built- in medicine cabinet. The medicine cabinet measures 2'- 0½" by 2'- 10¼" by 11" deep. The lower part of the cabinet is open, while the upper part is enclosed with a mirrored door measuring 1'- 7¼" tall. A small glass knob is screwed to the left stile on the door. There are two 2¼" decorative butt hinges on the door. A 3¼" frame surrounds the cabinet. Inside the cabinet are three ¾" thick shelves. Above the medicine cabinet is Door 17, which accesses the attic space. A towel bar is located on the west wall, at the foot of the tub.

Electrical and Heating and Cooling Fixtures. There is a ceramic, wall- mounted light fixture above the medicine cabinet. A duplex outlet is located on the north wall between the sink and the toilet.

The heating and cooling fixtures include gas service pipes located at the east end of the tub.

Room 114

Room 114 is in the southeast corner of the house, on the second floor. The overall measurements of this room are 11'- 9" by 16'- 4".

Ceiling. The height of the ceiling in Room 114 is 9'- 11" above the finished floor. The ceiling is newer gypsum board and is painted white. A 1'- 9" by 2'- 8" framed opening in the ceiling provides limited access to the attic. The opening is trimmed with mitered 3¼" by ½" framing and enclosed with painted gypsum board. It is presumed that the ceiling was installed by the Roswell Historical Society circa 1980s.

Flooring. The flooring is typical throughout this room except for one 5" board at the north wall.

Walls. The south, east, and west walls are plaster on lath finished with white paint. The lath measures approximately 1½" wide by ¼" thick. The north wall

FIGURE 75. Overview of second-floor bathroom, Room 113.

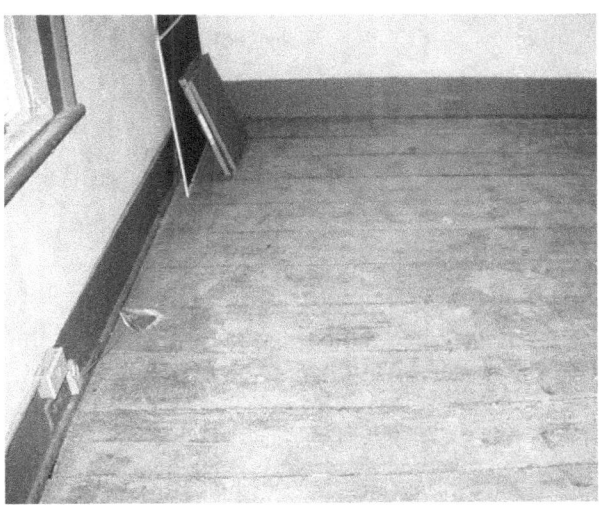

FIGURE 76. Flooring in Room 114.

FIGURE 77. View of closet (115) in Room 114.

FIGURE 78. Ceiling in Room 114.

is newer gypsum board, presumably installed by the Roswell Historical Society circa 1980s.

Trim. Molding measuring 2" crowns the walls. There are 10" wide baseboards throughout the room. A 1" quarter- round molding finishes the

bottom of the baseboard. The molding is unfinished.

Electrical and Heating and Cooling Fixtures. There are six recessed lights in the ceiling. Additionally, a ceiling fan with only two blades (two others are missing) is centered on the ceiling. These were likely installed by the Roswell Historical Society. Other electrical fixtures include six duplex outlets, one single outlet, and two telephone jacks mounted on the baseboards throughout the room. Three duplex outlets and two jacks are located on the east wall, and one outlet is located on each of the north, west, and south walls. The outlet on the west wall is located just above the baseboard. The single outlet is located above the baseboard on the east wall just north of Window 12. Electrical wiring conduit runs to this outlet along the east baseboard toward the north wall and along the north baseboard. The heating and cooling fixtures include two supply vents in the ceiling, along the east and south walls.

Room 115

Located on the west wall of Room 114 is a closet, Room 115. The overall measurements of the closet are 1'- 8" by 6'- 6" by 7'- 5".

Ceiling. The ceiling is beaded board, running north to south. Each board measures 3¼" wide with two ¼" beads.

Walls. The walls are finished with beaded board. The boards are horizontally installed and measure 3¼" wide with two ¼" beads. Four 1'- 8" by 1'- 3¾" by ¾" plywood shelves are supported by eight 2" by 1'- 1" by ¾" plywood brackets on the south wall of the closet. One 2'- 5" by 1'- 8" by ¾" plywood shelf is supported by two plywood brackets measuring 2'- 4½" by 3" by ¾" and 2'- 0" by 1¾" by ¾" on the north wall of the closet. A hanging rod is mounted below the north shelf.

Electrical and Heating and Cooling Fixtures. A ceramic mounted light socket is located on the east wall of the closet, north of Door 12.

Attic

Very limited access is available to the attic. Three accesses were located: 1) through an opening in the ceiling of Room 111 (the closet of Room 110), 2) Through Door 17 in the north wall of Room 113, and 3) through an opening in the ceiling of Room 114. In addition, efforts of the National Park Service to provide insulation for the structure have significantly reduced the amount of space within the attic. The reduction of available space and the covering of the floor surface made complete inspection of the attic impossible. From what could be observed through the openings to the attic, some of the interior walls of the attic are the historic, exposed plaster on lath. From the opening in Room III, 2" by 4", nominal studs, spaced at 16½" on center were observed. A foil radiant barrier has been installed in the attic, limiting a view of the roof structure. Additionally, a significant amount of cellulose insulation material has been blown throughout the attic space. The framing, foil radiant barrier, and cellulose insulation were installed between 2000 and 2002 by the National Park Service contractor. See the "Structural Systems" section of this report for more information on the attic.

Structural Evaluation

The contract for this Historic Structure Report did not provide for a structural evaluation by a Professional Structural Engineer.

Electrical Evaluation

The contract for this Historic Structure Report does not provide for an electrical evaluation by a Professional Electrical Engineer.

Summary of Materials Research Findings

The contract for this Historic Structure Report does not provide for a materials research investigation and analysis. However, in preparation for the 2000-2002 stabilization work by the contractor for the National Park Service, a mortar analysis was completed.

Physical Description

Treatment and Use

At the time of this report, the National Park Service had not formed a plan for the treatment and use of Allenbrook. The purpose of this report is to provide information about the history, chronology of development, and current condition of the property as well as some direction for treatment and use of the property based on these findings. This section outlines issues surrounding use of the building and grounds as well as legal requirements and other mandates that circumscribe its treatment. There follows an evaluation of the various alternatives for treatment and a description of the recommended treatment.

Research reveals that Allenbrook was most likely built by James R. King between 1851 and 1856, probably for his own use as owner of the newly-constructed Ivy Mill. From the time of its construction until its purchase in 1932, it was generally occupied by persons associated in some way with the Ivy Mill, later known as the Laurel Mill. The final private owner, Barnett A. Bell, purchased the house from the Georgia Power Company, which had purchased it along with the defunct Laurel Mill, probably for the purposes of demolishing the mill and building a hydroelectric power plant. Therefore, it appears that Allenbrook could be considered culturally associated more closely with the Ivy/Laurel Mill complex than with the Roswell Mills.

The significance of Allenbrook extends beyond its use to its architecture and materials. The building style is Plantation Plain. The use of brick rather than frame construction is rare for the Plantation Plain style. Though some modifications have been made to the house over the intervening one hundred and fifty years, the original style and configuration remains largely intact, a statement that cannot be made of many other homes of the same vintage. Therefore, the historic architectural significance of this house is apparent.

The National Park Service purchased the Allenbrook property to provide an entry and access to the Vickery Creek Unit of the Chattahoochee River National Recreational Area. The Park Service installed a small parking area east of the house, with a wayside map to the hiking trails along that side of Vickery Creek. The National Park Service has not determined a specific use for the house, though several campaigns of stabilization and rehabilitation have been completed since 1998.

Requirements for Treatment and Use

Treatment of the building should be guided by the International Building Code, including the code's statement regarding historic buildings as follows:

> **3406.1 Historic Buildings.** The provisions of this code related to the construction, repair, alteration, addition, restoration and movement of structures, and change of occupancy shall not be mandatory for historic buildings where such buildings are judged by the building official to not constitute a distinct life safety hazard.

Threats to public health and safety will be eliminated, but, because this is an historic building, alternatives to full code compliance are recommended where compliance would needlessly compromise the integrity of the historic building.

Applicable Laws and NPS Policy. Section 106 of the National Historic Preservation Act (NHPA) mandates that federal agencies, including the National Park Service, take into account the effects of their actions on properties listed in or eligible for listing in the National Register of Historic Places (NRHP) and give the Advisory Council on Historic Preservation a reasonable opportunity to comment. The National Park Service's "Cultural Resource Management Guideline" (DO028) requires planning for the protection of cultural resources whether or not they relate to specific authorizing legislation or interpretive programs of the parks in which they lie. Therefore, Allenbrook should be understood in its own cultural context and managed in the light of its own value so that it may be preserved and rehabilitated, for the enjoyment of present and future generations.

To help guide compliance with the statutes and regulations, the Secretary of the Interior has issued *Standards for the Treatment of Historic Properties*. Standards are included for each of four separate but interrelated approaches to the treatment of historic buildings: preservation, rehabilitation, restoration, and construction. These approaches define a hierarchy that implies an increasing amount of intervention into the historic building. The National Park Service's *Preservation Briefs* also provide detailed guidelines for appropriate treatment of a variety of materials, features, and conditions found in historic buildings. Regardless of approach, a key principle embodied in the *Standards* is that changes to the building be reversible. Alterations, additions, or other modifications should be designed and constructed in a way that they can be removed in the future without loss of existing historic materials, features, or characteristics.

Functional Requirements. The National Park Service has not determined a use for the Allenbrook building. Functional requirements would depend on the use to which the building is put, and should be defined at the time that use is determined. If the building is not open to the public and is interpreted in its current historic state, only maintenance is required. If opened to the public, access and safety issues, including fire safety, must be addressed.

Life Safety. When the National Park Service selects a use for Allenbrook, issues of safety must be resolved, both for visitors and for Park Service personnel. In its current condition, Allenbrook does not appear to present a hazard to human safety as long as the building remains closed to the public. If it is opened to the public, issues of fire safety

should be addressed, mainly those of egress during a fire and protection from live, exposed electrical wiring.

Security. Allenbrook is in a somewhat remote location and is currently unoccupied. Casual vandalism is reported on an ongoing basis. It is recommended that the existing alarm system be activated and monitored to prevent further intrusion. If the existing system is not a monitored system, a monitored system should be installed with the appropriate signage

Fire Protection. Allenbrook does not have an active fire alarm system or sprinkler system. The introduction of a sprinkler system to the historic building is not recommended. Such a system would have an impact on the rooms designated to accommodate the vertical riser, on the ceilings, and on the attic. Given the historic character of the existing ceilings in the building, the sprinkler piping would have to be installed exposed on the ceiling in the first floor, and either installed exposed on the ceiling in the second floor or installed in the attic with the sprinkler heads penetrating the ceilings. Operationally, running sprinkler piping in the attic would not have a significant impact on interpretation, but the negative impact on the historic ceilings to allow for penetration of the sprinkler heads or to affix the sprinkler piping to the surfaces would be notable. Therefore, unless there is significant concern of fire from vandalism or vagrancy, a sprinkler system is not recommended.

The following measures should be taken to protect Allenbrook and its contents from fire:

■ Smoke and fire detection alarms should be installed in each room, including all closets, the attic, and the basement area and wired to the existing alarm system.

■ Storage in the building should not include flammable materials.

■ The building should be locked whenever it is not in use, and should be under the supervision of National Park Service personnel or volunteer when not locked.

■ Contents of the building should be replaceable.

■ A fire response plan should be established using appropriate portable fire extinguishers and other support equipment, which National Park Service staff should be trained to use.

Energy Conservation. Allenbrook has a heating system, which is operational and should be maintained. Energy conservation measures were installed in the attic by the National Park Service during 2000- 2002 stabilization and rehabilitation activities. These are in the form of blown- in cellulose insulation between the ceiling joists and foil radiant insulation panels applied to the roof structure. The original plaster- on- brick walls provide significant insulating properties as well.

The shed rooms in the back of the house, where the ceiling has been removed, are spaces that still require some energy conservation measures. When the National Park Service replaces the ceilings in this area and reinstalls the molding, insulation should be placed in this attic area. However, any insulating treatments should not impact the remaining historic fabric of the roof structure.

Abatement of Hazardous Materials. Whether or not the building is open to the public, the building should be kept clean and free of bird and rodent droppings, which can be a health hazard. A Materials Analysis was not performed for this report, so the existence of remaining hazardous materials such as lead paint is unknown, but the age of the building and date of rehabilitation suggest that such materials might exist. A Materials Analysis should be performed at Allenbrook. It should include a paint analysis and a plaster analysis, at the least, to enable the Park Service to accurately replicate these materials for maintenance and repair purposes. A mortar analysis was performed at Allenbrook in conjunction with stabilization procedures undertaken by the National Park Service in 2000- 2002. In addition, the 1998- 2000 stabilization treatments included the abatement of asbestos- containing materials.

Handicapped Accessibility. The building is currently accessible in the lower level. All the major rooms of the ground level have door openings and thresholds compliant with ADA accessibility requirements. The closets and the bathroom are not accessible, and the entire upper level is not accessible. In the building's current configuration, handicapped access would be provided only through the front door, which has a threshold 1½" thick and is about an inch above ground level. A portable ramp would be sufficient to achieve accessibility at this location. The bathroom area on the first floor is only 6' by 5' with a 2'- 2" door opening, not sufficient for a handicapped- accessible bathroom, and it is not recommended that one be supplied. Pending a decision on the ultimate use for the building, it is recommended that the interior of the building not be accessible to the public, and thereby rendering full compliance with ADA requirements unnecessary.

The grounds of Allenbrook, including the parking areas, constitute a barrier to handicapped accessibility. To address this, a smooth surface for handicapped parking, with ramp access to the walkway to the building, should be provided, along with appropriate signage. The existing walkway appears to be sufficiently level to allow handicapped access, but vigilant maintenance is required to keep the brick surface from becoming uneven from encroaching vegetation and subterranean tree roots.

It is suggested that, to provide visual access to the rear of the building for the disabled, the access path to the Vickery Creek trailhead be resurfaced with a harder, level, and more durable material resembling the dirt path currently in use. If kept free of vegetation, such a path would not only enhance the visitor experience to the Allenbrook house, but would also provide better access to the hiking trails along the creek.

Alternatives for Treatment

Three main approaches to treatment of Allenbrook can be considered: preservation, rehabilitation, or restoration. Each implies a successively more aggressive approach to intervention into the existing building, possibly with a corresponding diminishment in the existing historic fabric. Preservation may not satisfy requirements for use, while rehabilitation may not facilitate, and, in fact, may diminish, opportunities for historical interpretation. Additionally, some historic buildings do not possess the architectural integrity to warrant a full restoration to their original conditions. In such cases restoration to a later period of a building's history can be the optimal approach to treatment, particularly if many of the original features have been lost. An examination of these approaches is useful in determining the best treatment for Allenbrook.

Preservation

This treatment would maintain the existing features and fabric by effecting timely repairs and routine maintenance, and by controlling the interior environment to prevent further damage from heat, cold, or humidity. Such activities would include replacing broken window panes, replacing roofing shingles with materials that match the historic as required, gently cleaning surfaces as necessary, and applying paint where appropriate to protect the underlying materials. It would also require repair of damaged wall surfaces on the interior and could include sealing of bare wood surfaces to protect them from further deterioration. Water damage to surfaces such as walls, ceilings, and floors would be repaired, and the source of the damage stopped if it still exists. The ceilings in the downstairs shed portion of the building have been removed. It is unclear what condition these ceilings were in prior to the 1998- 2000 National Park Service stabilization work on the roof. According to the construction administration documents, some finished ceiling materials were removed from these rooms, but the condition was not discussed. The exposed roof structure would be retained, and the ceilings would not be reinstalled because they are not vital to the preservation of the building. The existing molding still intact in Room 104 and that has been removed in Room 107 would be retained, and the removed molding would be inventoried and stored. The heating and cooling system would be retained and the automatic thermostat repaired to regulate temperatures within the building to mitigate spikes in temperature and humidity. It would not be necessary to replace the damaged ceiling fan in the upstairs bedroom, but, if not replaced, it would at least be removed and the ceiling repaired, as it is not significant to the historic character of the building.

If preservation were the recommended treatment, the building, most notably the interior, would not be improved or even returned to a previous state of functionality. The bathrooms would not be reinstated as functional. The National Park Service has upgraded the heating and cooling system during the 2000- 2002 treatments. This system would not

be removed. Likewise, the existing electrical system would not be upgraded, beyond what is minimally necessary as required for public visitation.

As discussed, the National Park Service has already completed an extensive program of stabilization and repairs to the building. The reconstructed portions of the building, such as the roof structures, foundation, and floor framing, because they are new, would not require more than routine maintenance. The most notable exception to this is the condition of the interior wall on the east side of the stairway, which would require substantial repair. It should be noted also that the investigation of this report was non- destructive, so the interior conditions of walls and other inaccessible features have not been ascertained.

While this approach would not diminish what remains of the historic fabric, it would also not improve the Park's ability to interpret the historic building. Currently, the presentation of the building, both interior and exterior, is that of an ante- bellum building adapted to modern needs and altered for structural stability, with features reflecting styles and tastes of the early to mid- twentieth century imposed upon those of the mid- nineteenth. However, some of the historic fabric has been altered and lost during the stabilization treatments. Interior and exterior preservation, therefore, as an overall approach, would be appropriate if the Park wishes to interpret the complete history of the building and its occupants to present day or to use it as a marker for the beginning of the hiking trails in the Vickery Creek Unit of the Chattahoochee River National Recreational Area, with no visitor access to the interior.

Rehabilitation

One of the most common approaches to the treatment of historic buildings, rehabilitation provides modifications to a building to bring it into better compliance with current building codes and expectations for creature comforts. With this approach, the heating and electrical systems could be upgraded to provide code compliance and human comfort. The kitchen might be reinstated, and the bathrooms might be made functional. All work would be designed to be reversible and would not diminish the historic building fabric or the house's historic character beyond the changes that have already been made.

Once a use has been determined for Allenbrook, decisions must be made about what period of historic significance to interpret. Whether a specific period is interpreted, such as the King family ownership of the building, circa 1851 to 1874, or if the complete history of Allenbrook is presented, rehabilitation would allow for a wider range of uses. Rehabilitation would also not require a strict interpretation of any one period, as this treatment focuses more on the ultimate needs for functional rather than interpretive use. However, as with any treatment approach for the building, rehabilitation must respect the historic character and fabric, as guided by The Secretary of the Interior's *Standards for the Treatment of Historic Properties*. Because rehabilitation would render the interior of the building accessible, the National Park Service could use the building for a number of functions. One option would be to provide housing for the Park's rangers, thereby continuing the historic use of the building as a residence. This option would also provide continued occupancy for the building, resulting in a greater level of long- term security and protection from vandalism.

Another option is to use the building as a classroom facility to host presentations to groups such as school children on nature outings, hikers, or those interested in the historic background of the Roswell area and textile mills. Incorporating the interpretation of the architectural elements of the building into this use would require identification of the known original features and the later additions, including an explanation of how and when things were changed, and why. This process would be a valuable educational tool, especially for younger visitors, to interpret how modern twentieth century householders adapted older buildings to their use by installing such amenities as an indoor kitchen and bathroom, electricity, and central heating.

Alternatively, the interior could be rehabilitated for administrative support. The Headquarters of the Chattahoochee River National Recreational Area of the National Park Service are located approximately three miles from Allenbrook, and provide office space for the Area's staff. If staffing space requirements are at or near capacity in the Headquarters complex, Allenbrook may prove useful in affording extra administrative offices. Alternately, locating auxiliary offices in Allenbrook may prove useful if a plan is developed to actively engage a continuous flow of visitors to the Vickery Creek Unit to learn about the natural and cultural history of the area. Such a plan may necessitate having one or more full- time rangers on- site, thereby mitigating the risks of vacancy. However, using Allenbrook for administrative office space may require significant intrusion into the remaining historic fabric to ensure the structural stability of the second floor, and is, therefore, not considered to be an optimal approach to rehabilitation.

Finally, consideration has been given to using the building as a house museum. While such a function could provide adequate occupation of the building, such a use would likely result in significantly higher administrative costs. Additionally, this use appears inconsistent with the existing programming and functional goals of the Park. Therefore, this use would be the least optimal approach to rehabilitation and not recommended.

Restoration

Not all buildings possess the historic significance to warrant restoration to a specific period. It is important to consider why treatment of this property should extend beyond preservation. The following discussion outlines the three reasonable options for restoration.

Option One. The first option for restoration is to return Allenbrook to its historic appearance before 1932, when the Georgia Power Company sold it to the Barnett A. Bell family. This period represents the building's association with the Ivy and Laurel Mills during the ante- and post- bellum years, especially through a succession of residents who worked there. Furthermore, this period embodies a direct association with the King family, notable for their role in founding Roswell and introducing the mill industry to the area.

Thanks to Barnett Bell's 1932 watercolor painting of Allenbrook, we have general knowledge of what the exterior of the building looked like prior to the Bell's renovations. The challenge lies in determining the original appearance of the house. No pictorial documentation of the house before 1932 is known to exist. However, some theories can be formed from the existing records of ownership and occupancy and from an analysis of the remaining material evidence. Current research revealed sporadic information on the likely occupants of Allenbrook from its construction date, circa 1851- 1856. After James R. King and family vacated the house, at least by the end of the Civil War, it appears to have been occupied by employees of the Ivy/Laurel Mill until at least 1905. The Laurel Mills ceased operation in 1911. Who, if anyone, occupied Allenbrook between 1905 and 1911 is unknown, but the residents, if any, were probably also employees of the mills. The residents of Allenbrook between 1911 and 1923, are also currently unknown. The Georgia Power Company owned the property from 1923 to 1932. Given the reported run- down state of the building in 1932, it is likely that the building was empty and no changes were made to it during this period. The basis for this assumption is the lack of information on occupants of Allenbrook during this time. It is reasonable to suggest that, given the circumstances surrounding the closure and dismantling of the Laurel Mills, the condition of the building by 1932, and the lack of available data on occupants from 1905 to 1932, Allenbrook may have been vacant during that time. In any case, the inhabitants of Allenbrook from the Civil War to 1932 were renters, not owners, and would have made few, if any, significant changes to the buildings. Until 1932, the owner of Allenbrook was always the corporation that owned the Ivy/Laurel Mill. It is unlikely that the corporation took much interest in improving the housing structure, and, therefore, improbable that they made any significant changes to it. The exterior appearance of Allenbrook as illustrated in Barnett Bell's watercolor is fairly consistent with the Plantation Plain style and shows the brick walls and stone foundation characteristic of the Ivy Mill buildings known to have been constructed by James King around 1856. Therefore, that which is depicted in the watercolor together with what we know from Barnett Bell's records and interviews about the interior of the house in 1932, is likely illustrative of the original appearance of Allenbrook.

A loyal interpretation of this period would require extensive restoration work, primarily on the interior. A materials analysis would also be required for the interior to determine some of the earlier and/or original finishes. Such an analysis was not included in the contract for this study. However, because Allenbrook does possess many of its original characteristics, returning to the pre- 1932 period is feasible. Returning the house to this earlier period would involve some change to its exterior, including the reconstruction of the one- story, front porch with the hipped roof on the front, removal of the back stoop and reconstruction of the original back door, where Window 5 now exists. According to the watercolor by Barnett Bell, the porch had four risers from ground level to the finished floor level of the building. In this watercolor, approximately twelve inches of foundation are revealed on the south side of the house, where they are now concealed by earth. The artist also included a depression in the ground level at the location of the porch, although it is unclear whether this was the actual configuration of the ground or an artistic device to allow for the proper depiction of the porch. Currently, the finished floor level of the building is only about two inches above ground level, and the ground then rises several inches toward the south, away from the front door. This indicates that grading of the front yard, including the addition of fill dirt, occurred after the removal of the hipped- roofed porch. The 1940 photograph of Allenbrook illustrates this change in grade. Re- instating the porch would likely involve removal of at least sixteen inches of fill at the south, or front, side of the building. It is possible that this removal could negatively impact drainage as well as the structural stability of the foundation wall on the south side. Archaeological investigation of the front yard would be required to more accurately determine the historic grade. While considerable site work has been done to the front and rear yards of Allenbrook, archaeological remains of the hipped roof porch footprint, as well as any other pre- 1932 site features, may still exist and prove important to the accurate exterior restoration of the building.

Additional changes to the exterior would involve returning the doors and windows to their historic appearance, consistent with the 1932 watercolor, and the existing shutters installed by the Bell family would be removed. Penciling on the north exterior wall would be applied to match the detailing on the east, west, and south exterior walls. In addition to the front yard, archaeological investigation of the rear yard and surrounding site could be used to determine the prior existence and location of historic outbuildings.

The interior of the house would require a large amount of restoration work to remove modifications made by the Bells and subsequent tenants. The stairway in the entrance hall would be removed, reversed, and returned to its original, steeper, narrower configuration, accessing the upper "loft" area without benefit of handrails. For this reason, visitors would not be permitted to the upper level, though it would be lighted to provide the opportunity to view it from the lower level. The entire upper floor would be returned to its original, open configuration, removing the later walls, plumbing, ceilings and bathroom fixtures. The walls installed by the Bells to create the bathroom and closets on the first floor would be removed and the rear hall walls would be extended up to the roof structure. The large, arched opening from the hall to the living room would be returned to its original size and location. Materials analysis of both the west wall structure of the rear hall, Room 105, and the east wall structure of Room 101, some of which might necessarily be destructive, would more accurately reveal their vintage. Specifically, comparison of the framing of the west wall in Room 105 with that known to be original to the house, such as in the west wall of Room 103, would likely indicate whether or not the former was a reconstruction by the Bell family, as theorized. Likewise, examination of the east wall framing in Room 101 may reveal the former location of the original door opening to this room off the hall. However, it is possible that the entire wall structure was significantly rebuilt at the time the Bell family created the arched opening, thereby destroying all evidence of the original opening. Materials analysis of the wall separating the front and rear hall may also provide more information about the approximate age of the door believed to have once existed at this location. If restored, a two- panel door like those believed to be original to the house should be hung in the opening. The opening to the dining room under the stairs that the Bells converted to a built- in cabinet would also be returned to its original state. As with the hallway, a two- panel door probably hung in this opening.

The plan of the first floor, while it appears that it was originally constructed as a central hall plan with two rooms on either side, is slightly irregular. The east and west walls of the first floor hall in the front of the house do not align with those of the rear shed rooms. The front hall (Room 102) is wider than the rear hall (Room 105) and the east wall of the front hall is slightly angled from north to south.

Additionally, the doors to the rear shed rooms (Doors 4 and 6) are not on axis. Door 2 is located on the southern end of the wall between Room 103 and the front hall. Given the location of the front door to the house (Door 1), it is highly unlikely that the original door to Room 101, west of the front hall was located on axis with Door 2 (see first floor plan on page 37). As it is clear that the Bells renovated a significant portion of the house, it is possible that they made further alterations to the downstairs than is currently known. Again, a detailed materials analysis of the wall finishes, and, if possible, the underlying structure, would shed more light on the original configuration of the floor plan and age of the existing materials.

Materials analysis may also reveal the earliest decorating scheme, if there was one. The architectural surfaces would be restored to their original condition, likely painted wood surfaces, with the exception of the floorboards. The floor cloth painted in Room 102 by the Roswell Historical Society is not based on historic documentation and would be removed. It is possible the finishes may have been more elaborate when James R. King occupied the building than they were when it was occupied by a superintendent or other worker of the Ivy Mill or Laurel Mill. However, this is pure conjecture. It is known, from the 1957 Atlanta Constitution article that the mantels existing in the house when purchased by the Bells were painted.

As described, restoring Allenbrook to its pre- 1932 appearance would involve some additional research into the finishes and features that existed at that time. Also, a large amount of material that has acquired its own historic significance would be removed from the house, primarily on the interior. Absent a current interpretive plan for the building, restoring the interior of the building to this period would preclude future opportunities to represent the later histories of Allenbrook. However, restoring the exterior of the building would prove valuable to the interpretation of a significant building style and period of growth in Roswell and Southern history. Therefore, while exterior restoration should be considered, restoring the interior of the building to its pre- 1932 appearance is not recommended at this time.

Option Two. The second option is to restore the building to the period in which the Bells owned the property, between 1932 and 1979, when Mrs. Barnett A. Bell moved out of Allenbrook, having sold it to the National Park Service in 1978. As of this writing, the historic significance of the Bell family is undetermined. However, it is known that Barnett A. Bell was an estimator for the Georgia Power Company, the company from which he purchased Allenbrook. As discussed earlier in this report, it is possible that the Georgia Power Company had interests in the Laurel Mill property because of its proximity to the Vickery Creek, with its potential for hydroelectric power. Apart from this possible historic association, restoration to this period would allow interpretation of a common trend during the twentieth century: the adaptation of older buildings to modern needs. The visitor would be able to see how modern requirements for conveniences such as indoor plumbing, cooking facilities, and electricity can be successfully imposed upon an older home without such facilities. This interpretive approach would allow the layers of history embodied within Allenbrook to be expressed.

Restoration to this period would require the removal of all renovations made by the Roswell Historical Society such as the gypsum board ceiling with recessed lighting, the ceiling fan in the upper floor bedroom, and the painted floor cloth in the lower hall. The bathrooms and kitchen would be reinstated, and architectural surfaces would be restored to reflect the pre- 1979 period. As with the first option, this treatment would require additional research to determine what interior surface finishes and fixtures existed in Allenbrook by the end of this period. Complete information was not discovered during the course of this research at the archives of the Park, but may exist elsewhere. The National Park Service has already largely restored the exterior of the building with a few notable exceptions. In rebuilding the north wall between 2000 and 2002, the National Park Service contractor replaced the bricks and mortar used by the Bells to close the back door with bricks and mortar matching those *original to the building* rather than matching those used by the Bells. If restored to the 1932- 1979 period, this treatment would be corrected, using bricks and mortar to match the historic pattern of the infilled wall. Several photographs exist that serve as adequate historic documentation of this feature. Additionally, the penciling found on the original brickwork, still

evident on the west, south, and east elevations of the building, was not replicated on the new north wall. This detailing would be restored using the east, west, and south walls as example. The two- story columned porch and the board- and- batten shutters that flanked the front door would be reconstructed according to their historic appearance. Both features are known to have existed in 1979, the last year Mrs. Bell occupied the house.

This restoration option would interpret the entire period of occupancy of the Barnett A. Bell family. Unfortunately, photographic documentation of the interior and exterior of the building in 1979, if in existence, has been unavailable to date. Many of the changes made to the building by the Bell family are known to have been undertaken shortly after they purchased the property in 1932. However, it is unclear what the full range of interior finishes was in 1979, when Mrs. Bell moved out of the house. Therefore, if this treatment option is chosen, additional research will be required to accurately interpret the period of 1979.

Option Three. The third option is to restore the building to the 1940 period. By this point in history, Barnett Bell had purchased the house from the Georgia Power Company and assigned it the name "Allenbrook." While it is known that some physical changes have occurred to the building exterior since 1940, it is that year which is easily identifiable through historic documentation. Information on the changes to the exterior by this time is supporting evidence that the interior modifications made by the Bells were completed by 1940. The historic significance of this year is that it represents a point in time when most of the physical changes to the building's historic character had occurred and that it allows for the limited interpretation of all of the building's residential occupants. As with the 1932- 1979 period of interpretation, restoration to 1940 would illustrate the twentieth century trend of adapting older buildings to meet modern needs. What distinguishes this period from the 1932 to 1979 period, for interpretive purposes, is the lack of documentation on the interior finishes and physical condition of the house during the later period. The 1940 photographs likely illustrate the earliest modifications made by the Bells to the exterior of the house. These exterior changes reveal that the interior first floor bathroom was installed by that time, as the rear entrance was relocated to the room now known as the kitchen. The written documentation from Barnett Bell, along with interviews from 1957 and later, indicates that many of the changes to the building were made shortly after the Bells purchased the house. It is reasonable to suggest that the Bells completed most of the interior changes by 1940, eight years later. If, as theorized, the building was vacant for many years, and knowing that the condition of the building was "run- down," these interior, modern improvements would have likely been needed immediately.

Restoration to this period would require the removal of all renovations made by the Roswell Historical Society, such as the gypsum board ceiling with recessed lighting, the ceiling fan in the upper floor bedroom, and the painted floor cloth in the lower hall. The bathrooms and kitchen would be reinstated, and architectural surfaces would be restored to reflect the 1940 period. Photographs of the interior, showing the living and sitting rooms, Rooms 101 and 107 respectively, taken in 1957 give some clue to the interior finishes. While it is possible that these differed from those that existed in 1940, some assumptions can be made. A materials analysis could reveal the actual paint scheme present circa 1940. Using information extrapolated from the historic documentation of Allenbrook, along with a materials analysis, a fairly accurate representation of the 1940 appearance of the interior of the building could be made. Interior modifications would include restoring the ceilings and crown molding to the shed rooms, reinstalling the door to the first story bathroom, reintroducing the first story bathroom and kitchen fixtures and possibly the door between the rear and front halls. Likewise, lighting fixtures such as the sconces on either side of the arched doorway in the living room would be reinstalled.

On the exterior, the second front porch with the gabled roof, the north wall with the infilled brickwork at Window 5, and the rear stoop with its simplified, metal hand rail would be restored. The brick hardscaping would be restored to the front and rear yards, preferably using any remaining historic bricks that exist.

As with restoring the building as described in Option Two, restoring the interior of the house to the 1940 period may prove premature absent a plan

for future use. Along with the materials analysis such a restoration treatment would necessitate, a significant amount of interior work would be required to return the architectural surfaces to this time period, resulting in added administrative and construction costs. Additionally, undertaking restoration efforts to depict the 1940 appearance may overshadow the earlier features of the house should an interpretive plan to illustrate the history of the King family, the later tenants of Allenbrook and the associated mill industry be established.

Recommended Treatment

Allenbrook is an interesting historic resource of the north Georgia area in that it is a *brick* Plantation Plain style building that has retained much of its original materials and configuration for more than one hundred years after its construction. While brick houses are not unusual to the Piedmont region of Georgia in the middle and late 1800s, given the readily available supply of clay, the articulation of this style, with elements of the Greek Revival style, is indicative of the upper class standing of its original owners. Additionally, elements of the building, such as the rear, interior chimneys are reflective of the northern building influences on the King family, who were originally from New England. More typical Plantation Plain style houses were of frame construction with exterior chimneys located on each of the gabled ends. Therefore, the opportunity to interpret such a structure in its earliest configuration is significant. Additionally, the connection of the Allenbrook structure to the King family, founders of the City of Roswell, and its continued affiliation with the local mills make it culturally significant to the area. The modifications made to Allenbrook on the interior did not completely alter the original historic character of the building. However, removal of these features to interpret the original floor plan would necessarily require further materials research and, ultimately, the removal of the circa 1930s finishes that have achieved historic significance in their own right. Without a prescribed future use for the building, a loyal restoration of the interior to the pre- 132 period may preclude future options and result in an unnecessary loss of historic materials. For these reasons, restoring the exterior of the building to its pre- 1932 appearance, while preserving the interior of the building in its current condition is the recommended treatment.

Allenbrook is a rare example of a brick Plantation Plain style, ante-bellum building, that exhibits circa 1930s modifications reflective of then-modern residential tastes. The National Park Service has yet to determine a future use for this structure. Therefore, the recommended treatment of the exterior and surrounding grounds will be considered separately from that of the interior as the ultimate use may allow treatment of these areas to be independent of one another.

National Register of Historic Places

Although not currently listed in the National Register of Historic Places, Allenbrook has been recommended eligible. Located at the southern end of the Roswell Historic District, which was listed in the National Register of Historic Places in 1974, Allenbrook is within the boundaries of the local Historic District. The District was zoned as the Historic Roswell District in 1971. At that time, the District did not include Allenbrook, but it was expanded in 1988 to include Allenbrook as well as a number of other properties. As discussed in *Roswell: A Pictorial History,* the Historic Roswell District "contains sites of natural or aesthetic interest that continue to contribute to the historic character and development of the City, County, State or region."[114] However, the National Register listing of the Roswell Historic District was never formally updated to include the expanded portion, so Allenbrook, while in the local Historic District, is not listed in the National Register. Despite its lack of national recognition, its historic association with the Ivy Mill, the King family (the founders of the city of Roswell), and subsequent mill superintendents and employees makes it culturally significant.

Furthermore, the building is architecturally significant for its Plantation Plain style rendered in brick, and its historic modifications, which reflect its continued residential use. The expression of the Plantation Plain style in brick and stone is unique, as the style is typically rendered in frame construction in the Piedmont Region of Georgia. Furthermore, the construction method is the same as that of associated mill buildings in Roswell, which were brick structures with stone foundations. The

114. Walsh, p. 173.

Historic Resource Survey of Roswell completed in 2001 by The Jaeger Company suggests that Allenbrook's remote location and the numerous non-contributing resources located between it and the existing National Register of Historic Places district boundaries make inclusion in a proposed National Register district expansion unrealistic. However, the *Survey* does indicate that the building is historically and architecturally significant in its own right. Therefore, it is recommended that this building be listed in the National Register of Historic Places as an individual resource under Criteria A, B and C.

Exterior Restoration: Pre-1932

The work undertaken by the National Park Service between 1998 and 2002 has stabilized and rehabilitated many of the building's systems and features. The following recommendations are provided to return the exterior of the building to its pre-132 appearance. The available research indicates that this period not only respects the historic character of Allenbrook but also offers the greatest opportunity for significant historic interpretation of the resource. These exterior recommendations are in addition to the general recommendations made at the beginning of Part II of this report regarding safety, security, handicapped access, and so forth.

■ The original porch, likely the hip-roofed porch, shown as a "ghost" on the front of the structure and illustrated in Barnett Bell's watercolor of Allenbrook in 1932, should be reinstated. From the historic watercolor, it is known that the porch had a hipped, metal panel roof, likely standing seam, wood posts, a wood plank floor, wood stairs comprised of treads and stringers, four risers high from the ground level to the finished floor and brick foundation piers. It is important to note that care should be taken when interpreting the historic watercolors painted by Barnett Bell, as some artistic license may have been taken in the depiction of the building features.

■ Restoring this porch would require the removal of the brick walkway and stoop installed by the National Park Service and detailed archaeological investigation of the area to the south, east, and west of the building to determine the extent of the foundations of the original porch and the accurate slope of the historic grade. This investigation must be conducted to a minimum of three feet below the existing ground surface due to the extensive ground- disturbing activities that the front yard of the house has experienced over the past seventy- five years. The ground to the south of Allenbrook has been re- graded to provide positive drainage away from the foundation and restoration of the historic grade may cause drainage issues. Study of this area will be required to assess the actual impact of restoration. If restoring the historic grade poses a negative effect on the drainage, it is recommended that the grade be returned to an approximation of its historic appearance while providing for the necessary features/ landscaping conditions to prevent damage to the house and surrounding area.

■   The existing front door should be removed and replaced by a board- and- batten door, as depicted in Barnett Bell's watercolor. According to this illustration, the hardware appears to have consisted of metal strap hinges.

■   Consideration should be given to restoring the windows to their appearance in the historic watercolors. In these illustrations, the sashes and sills are brown in color. It is unclear whether the paintings are depicting painted or unfinished wood sashes and sills. As mentioned above, artistic license may have been taken in these paintings, as is evident in the number of lights in each window. Barnett Bell has painted the windows to have only one fixed sash with six divided lights.

■   The existing rear stoop, porch roof, and rear door should be removed and the original rear entrance to the building restored to its historic location. The current rear door opening should be closed with bricks and mortar matching the existing in color, size, and composition. Restoring the historic rear entrance will require removing the center window on the rear elevation at the first floor level and installing one board- and- batten door and wooden stairs at this location. As illustrated in the historic watercolor, the stairs were devoid of handrails and simply constructed of treads and stringers seven risers high from the ground

level to the finished floor. In addition, the door hardware appears to have consisted of metal strap hinges. As with the front and side yards, archaeological investigation should be undertaken in the rear yard of the building to determine the accurate slope of the historic grade.

■   The brick and granite removed from the rear stoop should be retained. According to the Bells, brick (and, although they did not mention it, granite) was salvaged from the "the old mill" and used in the front and rear yards. It is reasonable that they used brick and granite from the same source when constructing the rear stoop. Though they did not define which old mill provided the brick, it is likely that they were obtained from the Ivy/Laurel Mill building ruins. These buildings were being dismantled by 1924. They were the closest available source of "mill" bricks for the Bells, and Bell could probably have obtained permission from his employer, Georgia Power, which owned the mill, to obtain them. A pile of bricks is also currently stacked in the basement of the house. It is unclear whether these bricks were salvaged from the site. However, these materials may be useful in the restoration of the exterior north wall.

■   Archaeological investigation should also be undertaken at the rear of the building to determine, if possible, the locations of outbuildings. It is probable that the earliest arrangement of this site included both an exterior kitchen and a privy. While not known to have been in existence at the time the Bell Family purchased the house, locating their remains, if existing, would aid in reconstructing the physical history of the site.

■   Consideration should be given to interpreting the historic drive that extended from Atlanta Street past the house. The 1978 survey of Allenbrook illustrates the configuration of this drive, and the 1940s photograph details its appearance. It was unpaved and lined with bricks set at a 45- degree angle. While it is known that the front, rear, and side yards were re- graded and paved by the Bell family sometime after 1932, the vintage of the entire drive is currently unknown. The entrance to the drive still exists from Atlanta Street. It is possible that this feature pre- dated the Bells. An old roadbed is known to have run past Allenbrook. This may have been a roadway between Allenbrook and the Ivy Mill. Future archaeological investigation may shed more light on these landscape features.

■ It is recommended that the National Park Service provide better access to this site for visitors. Currently, the entranceway is in disrepair, with deep ruts and missing pavement, and signage is inadequate. Handicapped access to the walkway is problematic. The vehicular entrance to this unit of the park should be re- graded and graveled or paved with a permeable material that complements the surrounding natural, wooded environment. If not governed by City of Roswell guidelines for signage, the entrance sign should be made larger and easier to read. Handicapped parking spaces with smooth- surfaced access to the walkway should be provided. Consideration should be given to hard- surfacing the access path to the hiking trail that runs behind Allenbrook to allow handicapped visitors access to view the rear of the building.

■ If the building is not opened on the interior to visitors, exterior signage or wayside exhibits could explain the interior and interpret the entire history and use of this ante- bellum building. The signage should identify the period of restoration of the building as pre- 1932.

Interior Preservation

To achieve a full interpretation of this building and its relationship to the history of Roswell, it should be made available to visitors on the inside as well as the outside. However, as the Park has yet to establish a future use for Allenbrook, the interior should, for the time being, remain closed. It is recommended that the interior be preserved in its current state to ensure that all remaining historic fabric is retained until a future use can be prescribed. This treatment provides for the continued maintenance of the building and the removal of only those features after the National Park Service purchased Allenbrook, that are not necessary to the stability and preservation of the building.

Sources of Information

Anonymous. "Background History – Allenbrook," unpublished research paper in the Chattahoochee River National Recreation Area Superintendent's Office files, date unknown, no page numbers. Much of the research for this paper appears to have been conducted by interview in the 1980s.

Bell, Barnett A. "Allenbrook," scrapbook relating to Allenbrook compiled by Barnett A. Bell and family. Contains two watercolors of the building as it appeared when the Bells purchased it, both signed by B. A. Bell, and several photographs of it after exterior renovations were complete. Located in the Roswell Historical Society Archives, Roswell, Georgia.

Braley, Chad O., Karen G. Wood, and T. Jeffrey Price. *An Archeological and Historical Survey of a Fifteen Acre Tract in Roswell, Fulton County, Georgia.* Athens, GA: Southeastern Archeological Services, Inc., 1992.

Brown, Lenard E. "Historic Resource Study: Chattahoochee River National Recreation Area and the Chattahoochee River Corridor," Atlanta: Southeastern Regional Office, National Park Service, 1980.

Census Records of the United States: Sixth through Tenth and Eleventh through Fourteenth, 1840, 1850, 1860, 1870, 1880, 1900, 1910, and 1920, Population Schedules, Cobb County, Georgia, and *Fifteenth, 1930 Population Schedules, Fulton County, Georgia.* Reviewed online at http://www.ancestry.com. These are scanned images of the original census pages.

Coleman, Richard G. "A Short History of the Roswell Manufacturing Company of Roswell, Georgia, Home of 'Roswell Grey'," unpublished paper in the Chattahoochee River National Recreation Area Superintendent's Office files, 1982.

DeVane, Ernest. *Roswell – Historic Homes and Landmarks, A Collection of Drawings* [with text by Clarece Martin]. Roswell, GA: The Roswell Historical Society, Inc., 1974.

Fulton County, Georgia, Gail D'Avino, preparer. *Assessment of No Adverse Effect to Allenbrook, the Robertson House, the H. S. Weaver House, the Roswell Historic National Register District and Ivy/Laurel Mill (Site 9FU228).* Atlanta: 1997.

Galloway, T H., ed. *Dear Old Roswell – Civil War Letters of the King Family of Roswell, Georgia,* Macon, GA: Mercer University Press, 2003.

Gerry, Maynita. "Confederate House is a Pleasant Home," *Atlanta Journal Constitution,* date unknown. Based on references in the article, it appears to have been written about 1953.

Hitt, Michael D. *Charged With Treason: Ordeal of 400 mill workers during military operations in Roswell, Georgia, 1864-1865,* Monroe, NY: Library Research Associates, Inc., 1992.

Jaeger Company, The. "Roswell Historic Resources Survey." unpublished report, 2001. Survey conducted for the City of Roswell.

"Meetings of the Stockholders of the Roswell Manufacturing Company, Roswell, Cobb County, Georgia, 1840-1900," unpublished, but bound, handwritten meeting minutes, Roswell Manufacturing Company Minutes Collection, DeKalb History Center Archives, DeKalb, County, GA.

Miri, Ali. *Historic Structure Assessment Report – Allenbrook House.* Atlanta: Historic Architecture Division, Southeast Region, National Park Service, 1994.

Mohr, Merri Ann. "Allenbrook Restoration Awaits Funding," newspaper clipping in the Roswell Historical Society files for Allenbrook, newspaper name unknown. Based upon the content of the article. it appears to have been written in 1983.

National Park Service. *Historic American Buildings Survey/Historic American Engineering Record (HABS/HAER).* Washington, D.C.: Library of Congress Prints and Photographs Division, 1936. Reviewed online at: http://memory.loc.gov/ammem/hhtml/hhome.html.

Richards, Alice. "Barnett A. Bells Preserve Charm of Circa 1830 Home," Atlanta *Constitution,* December 29, 1957.

"Rosters of Georgia Regiments for the Confederate States of America." Available online at http://

www.geocities.com/jshop24jhawkins. This website has links to rosters for both the Roswell Guard and the Roswell Battalion, with brief histories of each included.

Skinner, James L. III, ed. *The Autobiography of Henry Merrell, Industrial Missionary to the South.* Athens, GA: University of Georgia Press, 1991.

Walsh, Darlene M., ed. *Roswell – A Pictorial History,* 2nd ed., (reprinted in 2000), Charlotte: Fine Books Publishing Company, 1994.

Wood, Karen. *An Archeological Survey of the Presumed Location of the First Roswell Factory.* Athens, GA: Southeastern Archeological Services, Inc., 1989.

As the nation's principal conservation agency, the Department of the Interior has responsibility for most of our nationally owned public lands and natural resources. This includes fostering sound use of our land and water resources; protecting our fish, wildlife, and biological diversity; preserving the environmental and cultural values of our national parks and historical places; and providing for the enjoyment of life through outdoor recreation. The department assesses our energy and mineral resources and works to ensure that their development is in the best interests of all our people by encouraging stewardship and citizen participation in their care. The department also has a major responsibility for American Indian reservation communities and for people who live in island territories under U.S. administration.

NPS D- 74, December 2004
Chattahoochee National Recreation Area
Allenbrook HSR